THE POSTULATE
Mater Misericordiae
Merion, Pa.

Children's Shepherd

THE STORY OF JOHN CHRISTOPHER DRUMGOOLE

THE POSTULATE
Mater Misericordiae
Merion, Pa.

JOHN CHRISTOPHER DRUMGOOLE

Children's Shepherd

The Story of

JOHN CHRISTOPHER DRUMGOOLE

*Father of the Homeless and Founder of
the Mission of the Immaculate Virgin*

BY

KATHERINE BURTON

With a Foreword by

FRANCIS CARDINAL SPELLMAN

1826

P. J. Kenedy & Sons · New York

NIHIL OBSTAT: JOHN M. A. FEARNS, S.T.D., *Censor Librorum*

IMPRIMATUR: ✠FRANCIS CARDINAL SPELLMAN, *Archbishop of New York*

August 17, 1954

LIBRARY OF CONGRESS CATALOG CARD NUMBER: 54:10203

Copyright 1954 by P. J. Kenedy & Sons, New York

PRINTED IN THE UNITED STATES OF AMERICA

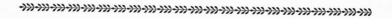

Contents

Acknowledgments

For their kind assistance in the writing of this book I should like to thank Right Reverend Monsignor John J. Corrigan, Mount Loretto, Staten Island; Reverend Edward Farrelly, Kingston, New York; Mr. P. J. Donoohoe, Scotch Plains, New Jersey; Reverend J. Franklin Ewing, S.J., Fordham University; Right Reverend Monsignor John M. A. Fearns, St. Joseph's Seminary, Dunwoodie, Yonkers, New York; and Sister Mary Loretta, St. Agnes Hospital, White Plains, New York.

Foreword

THERE is probably no other man in our country's history to whom we are more indebted for originating and developing our present system for the care and education of homeless, destitute, orphaned boys and girls than Father John Christopher Drumgoole, himself left fatherless when a young child in Ireland.

Father Drumgoole, founder of the Mission of the Immaculate Virgin, popularly known as Mount Loretto, in Staten Island, N. Y., was among the pioneers of organized social service in our country and was responsible also for many features of the system of vocational schools for boys and girls which is now an important and integral part of our present educational and training system. It was the vision, faith and charity of this true father to God's needy children that gave birth to Mount Loretto which, for over eighty years, has been a model child-caring haven for homeless, neglected children.

It was here at Mount Loretto, the "Mount Mary" of my novel, *The Foundling,* that the orphaned boy Peter, the novel's main character, attended school, found friends and was given spiritual guidance by the priests and Sisters of this great home-like training school. Upon it I patterned "Mount Mary," as so many child-caring institutions throughout the country are modeled upon Father Drumgoole's wondrous dream.

vii

THE POSTULATE
Mater Misericordiae
Merion, Pa.

No man has been a greater benefactor to society than John Christopher Drumgoole, whose compassionate understanding of the underprivileged was responsible for the establishment of this character-building institution wherein neglected, homeless youths are trained to support themselves economically and sustain themselves spiritually in the battle of life.

Father Drumgoole's spirit lives on in the life and work of every priest, Sister and lay worker of Mount Loretto. It lives, too, in thousands of children who have been sheltered and trained to become self-reliant, loyal and religious American citizens, and in the charity of those thousands of men and women who have generously contributed to the support of Father Drumgoole's providential Mount Loretto.

FRANCIS CARDINAL SPELLMAN
Archbishop of New York

August 3, 1954

‐≫≫

Prologue

WE SAT TOGETHER at a large round table in the dining
room of the New York Athletic Club. In the group were
one Monsignor, five businessmen, and one writer. The
Monsignor had brought us together in order to introduce
me to the others who were intimately connected with a
story I was planning to write.

Below us swirled the busy life of the city. Far off in the
sky an airplane was droning over our heads. Around the
table, over an excellent meal, we were discussing a man
who, in the early years of the nineteenth century, had come
as a little immigrant boy from Ireland, a man who was not
ordained a priest until his fifty-third year, and who died as
a result of exposure in the great blizzard of 1888. Yet he
had, in the less than twenty years of his priesthood, built at
Mount Loretto, on Staten Island, the wonderful home that
has sheltered many thousands of children.

It is a miracle of love today, as it was when he first
brought his neglected, orphaned, abandoned children
there. And it was built from nothing but faith in Divine
Providence, in Our Lady, and Saint Joseph in heaven, and
in thousands of the faithful on earth.

Only one of the men at the table was old enough actually to have known Father John Christopher Drumgoole,
but all of them had at one time or another lived at his
Home. I do not think I have ever heard anyone speak with
greater affection of his own home and of his own parents

1

than these men—all successful in business affairs—spoke of their foster home and their foster father.

Some months later I spoke at the Hotel Commodore at a Communion breakfast where everyone in the large gathering was a graduate of Mount Loretto. They had been sent to the Mission by those who wanted an orphaned or neglected child to have a real home. And they were all inordinately proud of being alumni and alumnae of Mount Loretto.

To the discouraged founder of a struggling congregation a wise old nun once gave sound advice: "You can never fail if you keep God in your heart." And this was the great secret of the success of Father Drumgoole: always in his heart was God—and God is Love. The great Home on Staten Island, just as much as the first plain shelter for newsboys and bootblacks in New York City, was built with love. The foundation was faith and love and that is why it has flourished. Next to God, Father Drumgoole put his faith in people and they repaid him a thousandfold, so that, incredible though it seems, the great houses at Mount Loretto have been built with the individual contributions of twenty-five cents a year which members of St. Joseph's Union sent him from all over the world. With it he bought land and equipment, and everything he bought was promptly paid for; there was never the shadow of debt on his Homes or against his name.

With this money he set up classes to teach his children to read and write, knowing the importance of education. With this money was carried out his plan for vocational schools, so that he may well be called a pioneer leader of that work in this country. With this money he first brought children from the streets, working children who, in the years before laws were made to protect them, often had no place to sleep save an areaway or a cellar entrance. There was always room in his house, for he was unable ever to turn a child away.

"He'll hang you up somewhere," said one boy who lived there to another who was afraid there would be no place for him.

This is the story of a successful life, the life of a man who began with nothing but love and worked all his life with that for his chief coin—the coin of the heart, which is pure gold. In a day when few cared, when the orphan earned a precarious living and went hungry if he did not earn it, when the poorhouse or the jail was the only place to put an orphaned or neglected or deserted boy or girl, he made a home for them and gave them the affectionate care of a father.

He worked with no fanfare, but he was known in many parts of the world before he died. His little magazine— *The Homeless Child*—was familiar in every country, for it was at one time published in five languages and by the hundreds of thousands. In only seventeen years Father Drumgoole amassed a fortune of more than a million dollars, but he died poor as he had lived poor.

At his death his boys and girls and his helpers wept his loss, for they all knew him personally. From others he had never seen came letters of sorrow, from high and low— from Italy a letter from Don Bosco, and from Father Damien in far-off Molokai a letter of sorrow at Father Drumgoole's death. From Rome came the condolences of Pope Leo XIII, who had hoped to see Father Drumgoole in person that very year. Over the years the priest had been given for himself and for his work fourteen blessings from the Holy See. He did not want to be elevated to the rank of domestic prelate when the honor was offered him because "it wouldn't help the boys," nor would he accept any decorations, saying: "What is to be given, give it to the Mission." When, through Cardinal Parocchi, was transmitted Pope Leo's desire to see him, Father Drumgoole answered that this was the greatest wish of his life, but he begged the Cardinal to explain to the Holy Father that he could not just yet leave his charges—"not even for a day."

He was often called a simple man, but it would be better to say he had great simplicity. Our Lady and Saint Joseph were the companions of his days, as much so as if they still walked the earth; it was they, he said, who gave him the resources all but limitless in amount that came to him and which were limited only by the great needs of his work.

In the spacious dining room of the club and the wide dining room of the hotel I saw the ripples of his love still reaching the shore. In his lifetime Father Drumgoole built good citizens and made unfortunate, helpless children into men and women who became the backbone of the country. And it is evident that, in his life in heaven, he is still carrying on that work of love.

1

⇢⇢⇢⇢⇢⇢⇢⇢⇢⇢⇢⇢⇢⇢⇢⇢⇢⇢⇢⇢⇢⇢⇢⇢

To a New World

THE OLD VESSEL creaked to her berth at the dock at Quarantine on Staten Island. Workmen caught the coiled ropes thrown to them and twisted them expertly around the piles. Over the worn railings hung the passengers, looking eagerly at the green, hilly slopes of Staten Island—a welcome sight after the gray expanse of sea which was all they had seen for weary weeks of sailing.

The voyage over had been very hard; deaths had occurred from ship's fever during the long passage; there had been a scarcity of food, and the immigrants to a new land had lived in quarters even worse than the poor homes they had left in the old country. But the memories of the days and nights on the tossing sea were behind them now, as the ship rocked gently in the lessening swells; and even further behind were the hunger and the bitterness of the old home. Ahead was hope, and the promise of a new life. New York lay before them, and the year was 1824.

Relatives and friends were waiting on the dock for at least some of the voyagers, though many among them now found themselves in a strange country where they knew no one. Those on shore strained to catch a glimpse of their own in the drab crowd where all the faces looked alike. A priest disengaged himself and made ready to board the ship, in his hand a list of girls and young women he was to meet and for whom he had made arrangements for decent lodging or for jobs in hotels or homes.

Off to one side of the dock stood a young woman whose blue Irish eyes anxiously searched among the passengers.

"I can't see him anywhere," she murmured, and there was panic in her voice. "Maybe he's sick. Maybe he's——" But she could not finish the sentence aloud.

The woman beside her patted her hand. "Now, Bridget, look at the hundreds of them up there. How can you find one tiny boy among them all until they begin to get off?"

But it was clear that Bridget Drumgoole was not listening. All her attention was fixed in her intent search for the one small face that mattered to her.

Then she saw him, perhaps because he had seen her and in his anxiety to attract her notice his waving arm moved faster than anyone else's. He was pressed tight against the railing, his brown eyes shining with excitement and his lips moving, but amid all the noise of shouted greetings she could not hear what he was trying to say.

The big push on deck began as one by one the passengers were allowed down the gangplank. To Bridget this was somehow the hardest part of all—to have to wait as the slow mass of people crawled along. The boy was so little that again and again she lost him from view, and was besieged by panic.

"Please watch he doesn't get hurt, Blessed Mother," she prayed, as she had so often during the past year, when the great sea separated them from each other.

A sudden little surge gave the boy his opportunity and he dashed down the gangplank, ducking between the legs of a tall man who began cursing the lad; then, seeing the woman and child run into each other's arms, he stopped suddenly and smiled.

Bridget Drumgoole knelt on the damp, splintery boards of the dock, her arms around her son, her eyes hungrily on his face. "But you've grown so, Johnnie, in the year away. You're going to be like your father, I can see that." For in his face she saw the close resemblance to John, her husband, dead these two years and buried in the village cemetery in County Longford.

Around them the crowds wept and laughed at their own concerns. The two had eyes only for each other. Finally the boy tugged at his mother's hand and together they walked to the pier farther down where a steamboat was waiting to take passengers to New York itself. John carefully spelled out the name on her stern—*Nautilus*—a lovely-sounding word even though he did not know what it meant.

All the way on the two-hour trip the boy chattered to his mother and she listened, hearing the loved little voice rather than the words. He talked of his leavetaking and told how Granny had packed big slices of bread for him to carry with him and managed to get him a couple of changes of shirts and socks for the boat. On the ship people had been kind, but he admitted that he hadn't had a very good time. She stole a glance at him, realizing fully the understatement of his words, for she had made the trip only the year before and she knew what it was like—dark holes to sleep in, food half spoiled, sick people all about, sometimes the splash that meant one more body consigned to the waves. He was such a little boy to have come alone. It was true there had been people on the ship who had promised to watch over him, and no doubt they had. But he had really been alone.

Johnnie chattered on, pausing only to stare excitedly at New York coming nearer and nearer, and its many buildings huddled down close to the water's edge. At last he could distinguish the men waiting to catch the ropes that would anchor the *Nautilus* to her pier.

He talked no more now of the voyage past, but with an eight-year-old's short memory he was already putting that all behind him. He fell silent as the ship reached the Battery and edged into Whitehall Slip. When they left the ship and were on the street, he was still quiet as he trudged beside his mother, carrying the cotton bag that held all he owned in the world.

They walked up The Broadway for more than a mile, past the rows of red brick houses. The Broadway was a fine street, thought John, but as they mounted he saw that the thoroughfares leading from it were only unfinished lanes. Behind him he heard a clatter of hooves on the cobbles and turned to see a two-decker stagecoach rattling along, the driver pulling on the reins, faces of passengers looking from the windows. The two passed a ship chandler's shop with its coiled ropes and capstans in the doorway, and a "medical dispensary" where globes held red and green liquids showing it was a place where drugs were sold. When they went by a little bakery, John looked at his mother pleadingly. "I'm awfully hungry," he said.

"Just a little longer. There's food waiting at home," she promised, and hurried him past a shop where the prices were beyond her slender means. When they came to St. Patrick's Cathedral on Mott Street, she hesitated. "It would take only a minute to pay a little visit," she said, "to thank God and the Blessed Saint for his care of you."

John nodded, and together they entered the Cathedral, one of the only two Catholic churches of New York City in that day. There was the other not far off, his mother told him—St. Peter's on Barclay Street—and another time they would visit it, too, for it was the oldest in the city and very interesting.

"This Cathedral was named for the great Saint himself by the Bishop of Baltimore who is the head of the whole church in this country," she told him. "And now they're talking of building still another church near here. Johnnie, you can go to Mass any time with all these churches so near. It is a good land, my son, and I'm glad we are here— and together," she added.

On the cornerstone outside the Cathedral John read: "Anno Domini 1809. Dedicated to St. Patrick, Apostle of Ireland." Inside it was cool and dark, and as he stared toward the altar the three naves of the church seemed to stretch out endlessly before him. But when they walked down the aisle hand in hand to the sanctuary, he saw it was because beyond the high altar a series of arches was painted on the walls, giving an effect of great distance.

There were two side altars, and John and his mother went to pray at Our Lady's, all white and blue, with little lights flickering before it. There they knelt side by side, and Bridget's heart was full of thankfulness and joy. How often in the months of their separation had she knelt in this church, beseeching the Blessed Virgin to watch over her little son, begging St. Joseph to father him. Her whole heart was filled with gratitude that at last here was her lad beside her, that now she could forget forever the black day when her ship pulled away from the shores of Ireland and he was left on the dock, so little and weeping so bitterly even as he waved good-by. Now they were together, and they would not have to be separated any more.

Beside her, John was remembering the chapel at home, and suddenly this big church and the city outside seemed overwhelmingly strange to him. He thought of the Killi-shandra Road to Granard where the chapel stood, and could see again the statue of the wounded pikeman which commemorated the stand of the United Irishmen against the English in the rebellion of 1798. His father had told him the story and had pointed out to him that on that spot men with homemade weapons had charged the most modern artillery of the day. "And for a good while held them back, too," he had added proudly.

He also remembered another day when his father had showed him the ruins of a monastery at Abbeylara, the little town in Coolcraff parish where John was born. "The town grew up around that monastery in days long ago," his father said, "and is named for it, too, for the old name was Lerha Abbey. And it was founded by St. Patrick him-self." And then he had told John many brave tales of the Saint, so that in the boy's mind the pikeman and St. Patrick were somehow identified, and as a son of Erin he was proud of them both.

And now this big shadowy church in America belonged to his home Saint, too. At first he had felt a sudden home-sickness, but now he turned to look admiringly around the fine building. So absorbed was he in this that he forgot even to say a Hail Mary. When his mother nudged him, he rose and genuflected, and together they walked out into Mott Street where he was going to live.

When they had come outside the Cathedral John stared about him with a child's curiosity. There were houses farther away but there were none at all around the church itself; it was surrounded by wide expanses of green grass and on one side was a quiet cemetery. "This part looks like country," he said.

"It does indeed," said his mother, "and last year a fox

thought so, too, for Mr. Idley—he's the sexton here—caught one right in the churchyard."

It was only a step from the Cathedral to her own rooms but they had to stop more than once because people came up to them with cheery greetings when they saw the boy beside Bridget.

"The lad's got here," said one. "Glory be, you have him safe," said another, and a third, "Now, Mrs. Drumgoole, you've got a man to take care of you, eh?"

Bridget said a few words to them all and John tried to smile politely, but he was really hungry now and wanted only to hurry home, and he was very glad when they finally came to the two clean little rooms, not far from the Cathedral, where he was going to live. There was a fire on the hearth, lighted by a kindly neighbor, and the kettle was steaming on the hob. John sat down thankfully to the simple meal his mother had made ready before she left to bring him home. It was very plain, but John opened his eyes at sight of the white cloth and white dishes, of bread almost as white as the plate it rested on. There was even, he saw, an egg that he hoped was for him.

Bridget put it to boil and made tea in the tin pot. Then they sat down together and John said the grace his Granny had made him promise to remember in his new home, and then he munched the fine-tasting bread and drank the hot tea and ate the egg Bridget had cooked for him. And together they made plans for the immediate future. John, his mother pronounced, was to have some schooling. He would go to the parochial school at St. Patrick's and maybe after school he could find such work as running errands. She herself had a job—housework for a fine family uptown who often let her bring home food. But the important thing, she made very clear, was that he must have schooling.

It made all the difference when a boy grew to be a man.

That night Bridget Drumgoole lay awake and listened with a thankful heart to the breathing of the sleeping child in his little bed on the other side of the room. The worry, the fears about him were gone now. Life would be hard, she knew, and they would be very poor. But they were together now; they were a family and not a mother and son with an ocean between them.

She heard the watchman's heavy step under her window, heard him pound three times on the curb, as he did each hour of the night, heard him call out, "Ten o'clock and all's well."

All was indeed well, she thought as she fell asleep.

Next morning, bright and early, before she went to work, Mrs. Drumgoole and her son John presented themselves at the parochial school so that he might be entered in his classes at once.

This school and the one at St. Peter's were the only free schools in the diocese, and had been set up by Bishop Connolly, the first bishop actually to occupy the see of New York, soon after his arrival in 1815. Since there was no building available at the time, he opened classes in the basement of the Cathedral, with two hundred and forty boys and girls in attendance. For a time he was forced to employ lay teachers for them all. He had tried to secure Christian Brothers for the boys but, chiefly because of lay trustee interference, he failed. With the girls he was more successful, for the Sisters of Charity, who had come at his earnest appeal in 1817 to staff an orphan asylum located in the Cathedral parish, were eventually able to send him Sisters for the school also. They lived close to the Cathedral on Prince Street, in an inadequate little frame structure which Bishop Connolly had promised to replace with a brick building as soon as he could afford it. In addition to teaching the girls in the school, the Sisters also taught catechism to all the children.

At first John felt shy at being thrown into this large group of boys who seemed to know so much more than he did of the contents of the books they were studying. But he found his teacher, Mr. Ward Farrell, a very understanding man, and before long John was no longer a stranger but one of a group. And Sister Elizabeth Boyle, who taught him his catechism, found in him an attentive listener, so much so that she promised to recommend him to Father Malou, one of the assistants at St. Patrick's, as a potential altar boy.

In the afternoons, when school was over, he hurried to a neighboring dispensary and spent several hours running errands for its owner. As his mother had said, there had been no trouble in finding work. The pay, of course, was microscopic, but it helped to keep the little home running.

In the evenings there was the joy of playing with the boys who lived round about. And right in the house was old Mr. Hennessey, who could tell the finest stories in the world. He had come from Ireland long years before, but his heart was still there even though the new land was long in his bones. He was proud that so many of his countrymen had settled in New York, and even prouder that the Irish had such a long connection with the history of America.

"In 1757—I read this in a history book," he told the children, "there was Irish soldiers right at Fort William Henry and they saluted St. Patrick's Day. And in the Revolution that you will learn about in the books it was the great Washington himself who gave orders at Morristown —over the river in New Jersey where he was camped—to celebrate the Saint's day. And right he was to do it, for didn't his wife's folks come from Ireland? She was a Ball and the Ball family was from near Dublin."

To John's delight, Mr. Hennessey had even known Granard. "In Longford County," he nodded, when John told him where he had lived. "Big people came from there, my lad. There was Oliver Goldsmith of the fine books, and Maria Edgeworth who wrote the tales about Ireland. And that was the place where St. Patrick and his friend St. Idus whom he made a bishop built the monastery, wasn't it? There's what's left of an old monastery there, too, eh?"

John nodded excitedly. "Yes, I've seen it lots of times." And the other boys looked at him with awe and respect.

One evening while the boys sat idly about Mr. Hennessey, waiting for a story, he said suddenly, "And do you know about St. Brendan who came to America in the long ago?"

Every boy sat up, and eyes grew wide. An Irish saint come to America? The old man smiled. "Certainly, and why not? In the ancient accounts you can find it all in a big book that I have read myself. It says he came to a land that he called 'Irland Mikla'—in the old tongue that means 'Great Ireland.' "

He stopped as if to refresh his memory. "He was an abbot in Kerry, this Brendan, and he sailed one day to the Isles of Aran to consult St. Enda about some traveling he planned to do. At that one's advice he set sail, and he directed his course to meet the summer solstice—and to know what that is you must ask Mr. Farrell," he said hastily, anticipating questions from his audience.

"No oar or sail had he as he went over the summer seas with his companions, but his ship went right along its course what with Providence guiding it all the way. And after a long time he came to a big stream—the Gulf Stream maybe, the book said, that is down in the south of this country. Then he landed in what the book says is perhaps the state of Florida, and he and the others left the ship in the care of God and marched for fifteen days, observing and making notes. And then came to meet them a tall man of noble presence, and he said Brendan had gone far enough and now he must go back home. He had completed his task and was to go to the Little Ireland and tell his people about the wonderful new Great Ireland. On the way home the ship was threatened with a great sea monster, as big as the boat, and some of the men, priests and abbots though they were, got very scared. But not Brendan. *He* sank the monster with a prayer."

Mr. Hennessey drew a long breath. "And when he got home he told the people about his discoveries and others made ready to go explore this land for God. And Brendan was so tired from his long journey that he had to take a long rest I suppose you think? Not him. The next year he founded a monastery of three thousand monks, the book says. A great man he was, eh?" And the circle of small boys agreed heartily.

Sometimes they sat listening to Mary Dermody, one of Bridget's friends, as she sang fine Irish songs in a sweet lilting voice. It was when she sang

> "Bells of Shandon
> That sound so grand on
> The pleasant waters
> Of the river Lee"

that John sometimes felt a slight homesickness for the town and river where he used to live, for Granard and the Killishandra Road and the fields, the green fields, of home. When he shut his eyes he could see himself back in his

Granny's house or, even earlier, sitting beside his father as he was cobbling busily at his bench.

Sometimes John and his mother sat in their own room and she read aloud to him from a book of poetry she had brought with her from Ireland. And, as St. Patrick's School made John more proficient, he used to read to her in turn while she mended his clothes.

One evening he found a poem about Irish immigrants and began to read it aloud to her:

"Each silent tongue held converse with the past;
  Each moistened eye looked round the encircling wave.
  We were alone on the wide watery waste;
  We were alone, the pilgrims of the sea."

He looked up and saw tears spilling from his mother's eyes at memory of that hard voyage. He went over to put a comforting hand on her shoulder.

"But we're not pilgrims any more, Mother, not now. We're Americans!"

2

꘏꘏꘏꘏꘏꘏꘏꘏꘏꘏꘏꘏꘏꘏꘏꘏꘏꘏꘏꘏꘏꘏꘏꘏

Boyhood in Old New York

LITTLE John Drumgoole's daily world was limited to Mott Street and nearby Prince and the neighboring streets, but sometimes on Sundays he and his mother walked farther abroad—perhaps to the Battery where New York strolled and watched the fine ships, or perhaps to admire the new City Hall now almost completed, or to look at the houses of the well to do on Bowling Green.

The city did not extend uptown much farther than one could easily walk, though in the other direction it was built straight to the water's edge where were the principal wharves and the seats of mercantile trade and the banking houses; at the upper end were homes of affluence and prosperous farms which extended past the Bowery Road. Between lay the houses of the moderately poor and the tenements of the very poor.

The New York of John's day was a city of great wealth and great poverty, of old families and new immigrants. In the early 1820s the settlement in the lower part of Manhattan which was the city proper held some 60,000 people, of whom 14,000 were Catholic. Already the city was spreading north as far as Canal Street, which had been at first merely a deep drain cut through a big marsh to serve as an outlet for Collect Pond. Now it was filled in and made into a thoroughfare, but the chief streets were still the Bowery

Road and The Broadway, the last two miles long and at least half of it paved. Between these two streets were unfinished alleys. The streets were lighted by oil lamps. Coal was almost unknown and hickory wood was the principal article of fuel.

The milkman came through the streets early in the morning carrying a yoke on his shoulders to which were attached the pails, and shouting, "Milk, ho!" Through the streets barrels of drinking water were hauled by horse and cart. Some of it was cheap and not very good; the best and costliest came from the Water Pump at Chatham Street and was sold at two cents a pail; painted at the end of the casks one read the words, "Tea Water."

With water so hard to come by, fire was something to be dreaded, especially in the narrow, closely built spaces of the lower town, but it was a fine sight for small boys to see the fire fighters in white coats and shiny black hats and the beautifully decorated fire engines, often pulled by hand over the cobbles. "Jump her, boy, jump her," the men would roar as everyone pulled hard.

In 1825, the year following John's arrival, many important events took place. Gas light was introduced and now lighted the streets below Canal; there was a great fete for General Lafayette in Castle Garden, formerly a fortress and now used as a reception center by the city of New York, when the citizens bade farewell to the lame and aging hero and warrior. But most important of all was the opening of the Erie Canal on November 4, 1825.

John and his mother stood in the crowd on the Battery when a fleet of steamers, all gaily decorated and filled with important guests, reached New York from Albany. The ships were trimmed with flags and the harbor was alive with large and small steamboats and hundreds of sailing craft. At the close of the celebration De Witt Clinton, who had been responsible for the completion of the great project, made an address and poured a keg of water from Lake Erie into the Atlantic.

Some days later one of the boys at St. Patrick's School told John that he had actually been on a barge on the new canal. If you wanted you could walk along the towpath, he said, and wait there until the lock filled up with water and then climb back in the barge again. And when a bridge came in sight the lookout shouted, "Bridge" and everyone ducked into the saloon till it was passed. John hoped fervently that his mother would take him for a ride on the Erie someday. But he knew that it cost money and there was very little of that to spend on canal trips.

In 1825 a fine new Catholic paper was published for the first time in New York and everyone was buying or borrowing the first number. A weekly, it bore the name *The Truth Teller,* and was published by Bernard Dornin on Pearl Street.

A neighbor had left a copy with Mrs. Drumgoole, and John studied it earnestly, from the date and motto on the masthead—"Truth is powerful and will prevail"—to the advertisements at the end. A woodcut headed the first page, a picture of Adam and Eve, both downcast and with heads bent, and between them an angel with a sword. The editorial was on religious hypocrisy, there was an article on England, Irish news with fine quotations from Daniel O'Connell's latest speech, a sermon by the French Abbé Papillon on the subject of the rich man who never says, "I have enough" but always "more—more," and a warning that the only money worth while was the gold coin of charity which would also be valuable currency in a future life in heaven. And there was poetry which John read aloud to his mother—stirring verses about Greece. Even the advertisements were poetical. The Fancy Store on Broadway had for sale:

> "Gold miniature fans and kid shoes in nut shells,
> Needle cases, scissors for natives or belles;
> Tooth brushes, pomatum and nail brushes small—
> If I counted till Doomsday I could not count all."

John could not read it all, of course, but under the tutelage of Mr. Farrell he was progressing well and managed to absorb much of the contents of the magazine. By the time it reached his house it had been in many hands and was much frayed, but it was a real pleasure to read of the life of New York there set down as well as of the wonderful things that were happening in the world outside.

Earlier in that same year of 1825 little John Drumgoole had attended his first important church ceremony in the New World—a sad event, for it was the funeral of Bishop Connolly of New York. There were many who mourned his death, for the Bishop had been loved by the members of the Cathedral parish and the other Catholics of his diocese. A member of the Dominican Order, he had acted as parish priest as well as bishop, always ready to listen to the woes of the poor, always ready to see the sick, and usually he had accomplished his errands of mercy on foot, for he had no money for a carriage. He was a man of plain tastes, which was as well since there had been little to spare for good living or elaborate ritual. A small, neat man, he had gone about his duties quietly but with efficiency. His rectory at 512 Broadway was a plain, simply furnished house. At High Mass he did not even use his miter or

crozier, but in his duties and the handling of his responsibilities he was every inch a bishop.

His task, of course, had been very difficult. He had, in a
way, to re-create everything, for when he came to fill his
see, long vacant, many of the institutions planned by
earlier missionaries and the Catholics of the city had dis-
appeared. And here was not only New York but the whole
of his diocese to be cared for. He had visited the whole
territory in those days of difficult travel and had provided
churches for the people in Brooklyn, Buffalo, Utica, Albany, and Paterson. By 1824 his health had been badly
impaired from work and worry. The trustees, realizing a
little belatedly that he had worked too hard, bought him
a horse and carriage and hired a coachman. This pleasure
—and he did enjoy it—was his very briefly, for only a year
later both his curates fell ill and died; while attending the
funeral of one of them, the Bishop caught a cold which
turned into a fatal pneumonia.

The body lay in state for two days in the center aisle of
his cathedral, and then he was buried close to the altar.
During those two days more than thirty thousand people,
many of whom he had aided with consoling deeds, words,
and prayers, came to visit his bier and say a prayer for the
dead prelate. He had by his kindly gentle ways made many
friends outside his own communion and some who came
were among these, one of them the Protestant Bishop
Hobart who had only recently made a trip to Rome and
taken with him letters from the Bishop to high officials of
the Catholic Church; it had been Bishop Connolly's great
hope to see this prelate a Catholic someday.

After Bishop Connolly's death Father John Power of the
Cathedral staff was named to act as Vicar General until a
new bishop was appointed. Even before a new bishop

could be named it became clear that there was pressing need for a third church in the city, for St. Patrick's Cathedral and St. Peter's Church on Barclay Street were overflowing, and Father Power knew he dared wait no longer to begin preparations for the opening of a new parish. When he learned that a Presbyterian church in Sheriff Street was for sale, he bought it for $7,500. It was a good building of wood with a brick front, and in its steeple hung a large bell.

This last was a fact worthy of note, for neither the Cathedral nor St. Peter's had a bell, and the new church—to be called St. Mary's—would be the first Catholic church in New York to possess one. The newly arrived Irish parishioners were especially jubilant for they had grown used to having no bells in their churches, since the British government had decreed that their chapels must be built without spires.

The church on Sheriff Street was opened in 1826, in Our Lady's month, since it was to be dedicated to her. There was great excitement on Grand Street and in the neighborhood when the bell was rung for the first time. To the children it was just a pleasant sound. To some of the older people it was a peal of joy and triumph, and as its echoes were heard in Delancey Street and Sheriff and Grand, men and women stopped to listen, and many had tears in their eyes.

The church was to be dedicated as soon as the new bishop arrived. Already there were unhappy rumors as to who this would be. The people of the diocese hoped it would be Father Power, but word was spreading that Archbishop Carroll was considering a priest from Maryland—Dr. Dubois, a learned man with a reputation for organization—but French!

The news proved to be true. In 1826 Dr. Dubois was appointed and Father Power was made pastor at St. Peter's. The disappointed Catholics were happy that at least he would remain with them. As for the newcomer, there was much muttering about him from the more excitable of the Irish.

As Bridget Drumgoole came home from work on the day the news arrived of the new appointee, John heard a neighbor call to her, "The man where I work says the people will let the new bishop come but afterwards they'll give him trouble because he's somebody that's been intruded on them by undue influence."

"But why would they do that?" asked Mrs. Drumgoole.

"He's a foreigner," said the other woman distrustfully. "He comes all the way from France."

"But you and I came all the way from Ireland," said Mrs. Drumgoole reasonably.

The other woman was not convinced. "It's different entirely," she said.

The man about whom so many tongues were wagging had come from France during the Revolution and had been in the Maryland diocese ever since. He had founded Mt. St. Mary's College at Emmitsburg and had expected to end his days there. Already sixty-three years old when the bishopric was offered to him, he had reluctantly accepted it. When he came to New York from Baltimore after his consecration, ready to work hard at the task, he found only two priests at St. Mary's, one at St. Peter's, and two at the Cathedral. He was not daunted by this. He had been a missionary priest and had always worked hard. "I am bishop and parish priest and catechist," he wrote cheerfully to a friend in Lyons, adding that he had 35,000 Catholics in the city alone, with three churches, and would

soon have a fourth, which was to be named Christ Church.
He had brought with him from Maryland three young
priests to help with the religious instruction of the children
and hoped he would be allowed to keep them.

It was, in fact, the condition of the children of the city
which had especially appalled him after his first months in
the city. The one Catholic orphan asylum could not take
in half the applicants. There were no charitable associations to help, and few nuns. Catholic children whom the
asylum could not take or who were friendless or without
relatives were left to the Protestant missions, to the poorhouse, or to the hard kindness of the streets.

Bishop Dubois was well aware that he was not the choice
of his new see. He was an outsider and a Frenchman. He
tried to disarm the members of his flock in his first pastoral
letter when he wrote, almost pleadingly, "We, too, are
American. But we are all Catholics. Are not distinctions of
birth and country lost in this common procession?" And
he divulged his plans for the diocese, carefully and fully,
even though he feared they would not meet with much
friendly approval. He knew well how its three churches
were like a bit of Ireland itself to the weary wanderers who
came, tired, sick, poor, on the ships from the old land. He
tried to please them as best he could, as with his gesture in
1829 of ordering a *Te Deum* sung in each church as a
thanksgiving for Catholic Emancipation in Ireland.

That year he went to Rome to ask for advice on his
difficult new assignment. He collected money in various
countries in francs and gulden and marks, but his chief
hope was not fulfilled: he was not able to recruit more
priests for his ever-growing flock.

In 1826, under the patronage of Dominic Lynch, a well-
known merchant of New York, the famous Garrica troupe

of singers gave a concert at the Cathedral for the benefit of the orphan asylum on Prince Street. Many outsiders came, and the fine sum of five thousand dollars was realized.

Young John and his friends had no money for tickets but as they stood close to the church walls and listened to the lovely strains John wished he could sing like these Italians. When he reached home he learned that all the strains had not been lovely.

"The Cathedral choir is very angry," a neighbor was telling his mother. "They think they should have been asked to sing, too. And they think that maybe they won't sing at all next Sunday."

Mrs. Drumgoole smiled at that and so did her visitor. And on Sunday John, who loved singing and had been really alarmed at this threatened strike, heard the familiar voices singing placidly and with no hint of past dissension.

John Drumgoole was particularly attached to one of the priests brought by Bishop Dubois from Maryland and now serving as an assistant at St. Patrick's Cathedral. This was Father Malou, the romantic story of whose past was recounted with relish by his parishioners.

In his native land Father Malou had been a general of the army and had planned to retire and settle in America. He had come alone, meaning to send for his wife as soon as he found a good home in New York, but he was in the city only a short time when he received word of her death. In deep grief he returned to Belgium, saw that a monument was erected in his wife's memory, and settled his affairs; then he entered the Jesuit Society as a lay brother, his identity known to none of the members of his community. One day when he was at work in the garden his superior appeared with a group of military officials. Suddenly the group halted, and to the superior's surprise he saw they were saluting the gardener who gravely returned their salutes. The new lay brother was distressed at having been recognized, but, at the insistence of his superiors, he agreed to enter the seminary and become a priest, and later he was sent to the New World.

Everyone at St. Patrick's liked Father Malou very much —his grave dark face which lighted up with a smile when one of the children approached him, his odd use of English, his kindness with the small difficulties of a child. It was a sorrow to them all when he died in 1827. He was buried in the crypt of the Cathedral. He had tried hard to make good altar boys of some of the younger children— John Drumgoole among them. Sister Elizabeth Boyle helped, too, with this good work, and the Cathedral was known in the city for its excellently trained acolytes.

During the years that John Drumgoole was growing from a little boy to a self-reliant youth the thought of becoming a priest had often come to him. There were many things to foster it and several people had helped—Father Malou who had said Mass so reverently that it held the attention of even a very young server, the wonderful stories that Sister Elizabeth Boyle had in her repertory, his mother's deep devotion to the Faith—so that the growing lad's thoughts were often on the priesthood.

But, as John grew older, though the desire increased, the possibility became more remote. He knew in his heart that there was little chance of that for him. Funds for the education which such a future demanded were very limited— in fact, all but non-existent. Between them he and his mother barely managed a very simple living.

John's days of errand running ended when he was offered a job to help a shoemaker on Mott Street after school.

Small child that he had been when his father died, he had
learned from him a little of the trade and it proved helpful
in getting him the job. By the time he was about fourteen
years old, the rising costs of even their simple living had
made it clear that he must earn more money. Despite his
mother's reluctance and his own regret, he left school and
took on the work of cobbling. Before long he was the
virtual breadwinner of the family.

One evening in 1831 Mrs. Graves, who lived next door,
came breathlessly into the room where the Drumgooles
were eating a quiet supper. "Saints have mercy," she
gasped. "St. Mary's is burned to the ground and they say
Father Barry is so shocked that he's been put to bed by
doctor's orders."

It was all sadly true, and feeling ran high in the neighborhood, even higher when it was discovered that the
church had been robbed and the clapper of the bell tied
so that it could not be rung as an alarm. The inadequate
fire engines, the pails and pails of water had proved un-
availing. Later investigation showed that the building had
been set on fire in three places, so that the arson appeared
to have been carefully planned. And the safe, which was
all that was saved, was found to have been rifled.

That night there were angry words uttered through the
parishes, for many thought the incendiaries were anti-
Catholic fanatics. This was no unreasonable fear, since
with the years the feeling against Catholics in the large
cities had grown. More and more bigotry was being shown
against the increasing Catholic population, due to a constantly growing number of immigrants in Philadelphia
and Boston as well as in New York.

In earlier days there had been a much more friendly

spirit. Protestants and Catholics in America were wont to act together. As late as 1826 St. Patrick's Day was celebrated in Brooklyn by Irishmen of both creeds, all of them marching to St. James' to Mass and then attending a banquet presided over by a Methodist minister. Now things were changing and with an increasing and alarming speed, and the group which was to grow into the Native American organization was forming.

Attacks on the Catholic population were extending to the pages of the press. One violent editorial said they were "coming hither with hasty strides to take the whole land." To such remarks Catholics made equally vigorous protests, but the attacks grew wilder and more gross. "It was the time of the tomahawk in literature as well as in war," wrote a chronicler of the period.

When the excitement over the fire at St. Mary's had subsided, the parish considered plans for rebuilding. From his sickbed Father Barry offered suggestions for a new church, but he thought for the immediate present it might be wise to lease temporarily a small wooden building on Grand Street, the abandoned property of the Episcopal Church. This would do for the time being, and meantime St. Mary's could buy lots and build a church of its own. But he did not live to follow up his plans. Only a few weeks after the fire had destroyed his beloved church, Father Barry died.

After his death, Father McGuire, his assistant, in consultation with the trustees, rented the old church on Grand Street, as Father Barry had suggested. It was decided not to build on the old site but to buy three lots on Grand Street and there erect a new church. At the same time Bishop Dubois presented the parish with a lot on which to build a rectory, and he himself laid the cornerstone for the new church in 1832.

But the completion of this building was very slow. It was in that year that a terrible epidemic raged in New York. Builders were few; money was hard to find, since the means of many people were being expended for sick care or funeral expenses. In one day from one house in St. Mary's parish five coffins were carried.

By late December of 1832 the basement was ready and the first Mass was said. The Bishop dedicated the new church in June of 1833. In the autumn a school was opened, also in the basement, and the Sisters of Charity came to staff it.

By this time Bishop Dubois, old, weary, and sick, had been persuaded to semi-retirement, and for some years he let the younger men do most of the work. Despite the grumbling about the Bishop, some of which had really never ceased, he had done excellent work for his diocese. But he had never, despite his efforts, become popular. He had not wanted to come to New York at all; he had wanted to stay the rest of his days at his beloved Mt. St. Mary's. No doubt he had not fully realized the resentment of the Irish against him, and it was also true that despite his thirty-five years in American church work his accent still made it sometimes hard to understand him.

The trustees made his later years difficult, too. At one point they threatened to cut off his salary if he did not appoint the priests they wanted. This time the old man wrote a letter to his tormentors: "I have seen the horrors of the French Revolution and could meet them again. I am an old man. I can live in a garret or a cellar, but, gentlemen, whether I come down from my garret or up from my cellar, you must remember that I am still your bishop."

By 1837 he had known that he could no longer carry on his work and asked for a coadjutor. He was given Bishop John Hughes, himself an old Mt. St. Mary's student, and there was rejoicing among the Irish at the selection. By 1838 Bishop Dubois had turned over nearly all his duties to the younger man. After suffering a stroke, he gave entire authority to Bishop Hughes. "I obey the bit," he said, "but not until I have covered it with foam."

3

⇛⇛⇛⇛⇛⇛⇛⇛⇛⇛⇛⇛⇛⇛⇛⇛⇛⇛⇛⇛⇛⇛⇛⇛⇛⇛

The Sexton of St. Mary's

IN HIS HEART John Drumgoole still carried the hope that
had been with him since boyhood and which he had
shared with few. Since his years as altar boy at St. Patrick's,
his desire to serve God as a priest had remained warm and
living within him, and he still hoped that someday what
looked impossible could be accomplished. He knew well
the difficulties of bringing his hope to actuality. For one
thing, his mother could add but little to the common
fund, as she was less and less able to do the hard work
which was the only kind she could procure. There were
various relatives in the country, of course—Leveys and
Reillys and Drumgooles—but John knew none was well
off and all had their own to care for, their own bills to
meet. But he knew, too, that the will of God could move
mountains. He waited patiently; he said little. But during
the years of his youth he never ceased to hope.

Meantime he worked cheerfully at his daily tasks and
put his future in the hands of God.

November 7, 1838, was a very important day for John
Drumgoole. It was the day he was to receive his citizenship
papers.

Early that morning he went to the New York Marine

Court where he passed the test to prove he could speak English and read it. And then he took the oath of loyalty to his country.

When he brought home his certificate of citizenship, his mother studied the document carefully and proudly. It bore not only the seal of New York but the great seal of the United States; its legal phrases were written in a handsome copperplate script and under her son's name in large letters appeared the words: "A citizen of the United States."

Mrs. Drumgoole put the paper carefully away in the big Bible. When she turned, she saw that John was standing looking pensively out of the window.

"You think you own the land now, I suppose," she said jokingly.

He looked at her solemnly and with no trace of an answering smile. "But it is true, Mother," he said. "I do. I really am one of the people who own it now. I pray that I will be an honor to it and never disgrace it in any way."

Finally, in 1844, John was able to leave his job of cobbler to take work that was very much more to his taste. He had been appointed sexton of St. Mary's Church. It was not by chance this position had been offered to him, for John Drumgoole was known among his own people for his devotion to his faith. Early churchgoers found him always at the early Mass, his beads and missal in one hand, in the other a candle to light the pages of the book. He had been chosen by a pastor who knew him well and who thought he would be a good influence, especially among the younger parishioners.

John and his mother moved from Mott Street to a house near St. Mary's so that he might be nearer his duties. Between them they managed well, for she found light work in the neighborhood.

At St. Mary's John often served the Masses, and he also helped train the altar boys. He aided with the catechetical instruction and taught in the Sunday school. In an effort to keep the children from the streets, he organized several clubs for boys which met in the evenings. When missions were held in the parish, he often went after stray sheep whom he knew personally and begged them to come. From the docks he brought longshoremen to the mission, having first made certain that seats in the church were reserved for them.

Himself devoted to Our Lady and knowing the extent of this devotion among many others in the parish, he asked Father Starrs, then the pastor, whether they might have May devotions at St. Mary's. When he made this request he showed Father Starrs a book by Father Faber and pointed out to him one particular sentence: "Can we help a certain jubilee of heart in thinking that the month of God's mother has now begun?" These devotions were started and soon became very popular. It was directly due to their celebration in St. Mary's parish that four years later they were begun in various other churches in the city.

It was during his first years at St. Mary's that he became aware, through his work with the boys who came to the church for religious instruction or whom he had seen running about the streets and had never seen inside the church, of a condition he had as a child and a boy merely accepted—the grinding poverty of so many of New York's people—a poverty that brought illness and death to many breadwinners and left thousands of small children homeless and unprotected.

He could not, of course, know the whole picture of the day, its entire blackness, but St. Mary's immediate neighborhood gave him a great deal to brood over. He himself was the child of poverty but at least he had always had a home and the devoted love of a mother. He had gone to the parochial school where the early teachings of his mother had been supplemented by the Sisters and the priests. Now he realized how many little children knew nothing of home or cleanliness and nothing at all of God. And many of them were the children of Catholics, little fragments from the body of Irish faith. Now and then young members brought to the clubs for boys which he had set up some friend of the streets and it was through them that he came to know the problems that faced society and especially the Church to whom many of these children belonged. These problems, he knew, were largely the result of the tides of Catholic and Irish immigration that had swept the country in recent years.

During the 1830s and to the middle of the 1840s this immigration had lessened somewhat, for a spirit of optimism had prevailed in Ireland after the Catholic Emancipation Act of 1829. In the United States the Friends of Ireland were formed; much money was sent to help that country, but in the end only disappointment resulted. All the wisdom of O'Connell was of no avail, and by 1847 everyone knew it, and money was again being sent to relieve the latest and worst of Irish famines. Reports of conditions were beyond belief even to those who had once known poverty there. It was said that two thirds of all manufactories were closed; people were in rags, fed on half-rotten potatoes, lodged often in sties.

When actual deaths from hunger were reported, the Irish-born in America were not the only ones who hastened to help. From Catholic and Protestant pulpits alike came pleas to aid the starving land. The American government sent two ships of war loaded with food and clothing for the sufferers. But all the generous gifts fell short of the terrible need.

The result of this was an increase in immigration to the United States on the part of those who could raise the money by selling what they had in the Old World or by begging passage money from their more fortunate relatives in the New World. Many of those who came were weak and sick from deprivation, and the hard voyage had made their condition worse. Often parents died on shipboard or after landing, and their children were left without relatives or friends in a city that already had more than it could care for.

Many charitable persons helped in whatever way they could, some with money, some trying to find a place where these children could be housed and fed. Among these was John Drumgoole, who could help only in a small way, although he did what he could. Often he allowed the homeless waifs of the street to gather around the heater, in the basement of the church, and sleep. He rounded up children who had lost their parents and tried to find at least a temporary home for them; he worked with the boys in the clubs he had formed and found food for them when they were hungry. Still he knew that he was touching only the very edge of a terrible and constantly growing problem, and he considered with grave concern these guttersnipes, many of them clever, bright-eyed, independent, but already old in knowledge of the worst side of life and with little information about the better side.

He told himself, coming home at night after locking up the church, or when on Grand Street or Delancey he saw homeless children asleep in the corner of a building or in an areaway, that someday he would try to extend his little clubs to other parts of the city. He began to dream of clubs all over New York, where religion would be made attractive to the children and where they would find help for their physical needs, perhaps even a house where they could sleep at night, one where they could get some education and training for a trade. Some of them were such bright little fellows and they ought to be made an asset to their country and not spend their adult days in jail for crimes.

And then, after such grandiose plans, he would smile sadly to himself—the sexton of St. Mary's, himself untrained, himself poor, daring to have such thoughts. He tried to put them out of his mind, but the hopes and the plans always came back when he met a friendless, homeless child, asleep in the street, unsold newspapers folded under his head for a pillow or his shoeshine kit under his arm so that it would not be stolen while he slept.

Then, too, John Drumgoole realized it was not only the children who needed help; it was the grown people also. The immigrants from the incoming boats who were crowding the city had another enemy besides poverty: ignorance and lack of education, either formal or in a trade. He saw the great need of adult schools for these people, places where they could come at night to learn. He had found among them some very eager to study, eager to better themselves—but how? Who would help to give them the opportunity? Some could read fairly well, of course, but even the available books were too costly for those whose little money must go for food and shelter.

For some time John Drumgoole had realized that the time had come for him to seek advice regarding his ambition to enter the seminary. The deep hope was still with him, but he knew that soon he must give it up or bring it to fruition, for he was growing toward middle age. Soon he would be too old to be received as a student. Then, too, he must study a great deal before he could even enter a seminary. The time had come to speak to someone, but whether to consult his pastor or someone else he was not certain. In the end it was to his pastor that he presented his problem.

When he did so Father McCann looked at his sexton keenly. John was about thirty years old now, strong and healthy. His dark eyes were full of intelligence, his mouth showed a firm will, his forehead was high under the dark hair. The pastor hesitated as to what to say to the man before him, for he felt grave doubts that he would be able, at his age and with so little education, to become a priest.

"But you are not young any more," he began hesitantly, "and to begin the life of a seminarian now—— and, besides, the Latin alone may be a great problem—— and then, John—the money——"

"I know, I know," said John despondently, and then, in a firmer voice and as if pleading his cause, "but I think that God wants me to be a priest."

"Well, if He does, He will bring it about," said the pastor, but there was not much in his voice to encourage his sexton. In fact he had been greatly amazed to learn of John's desire. He had never once guessed that his faithful worker had any such aim.

A second talk on the subject disclosed the fact that John was thinking of becoming a monk.

"No, no, John, surely your work is in the world. Look, man, how would you like it if you had no boys to fuss with, no clubs for them? No, John, stay in the world. The boys need you. And you go talk the whole thing over with your mother," he added. "She is a sensible woman. See what she thinks."

That evening, when the boys had gone home and he had carefully locked up the church, he went home to talk with his mother. She had, of course, been long aware of his great desire; he had never been able to conceal it from her entirely. But she had thought of it as a vague idea in his mind which would remain just that. Now, almost with a shock, she realized how deep was his yearning, how firm his convictions about his future.

She did not hesitate even for a moment. "Then you must do it, John. I can't help you with money but I can pray for you and I can live somewhere else so that you can save your money faster."

But such a solution, he assured her, had never entered his head. "No, before I go I want to save enough for your keep while I am away," he said. "I can do it. But I'm going to begin to study right now. I'll take some courses at St. John's College at Rose Hill and, if the pastor thinks well of the idea, I'll take what I've saved so far and open a little bookstore across the street from St. Mary's and make some money that way."

At 443 Grand Street he opened his little shop. He spent his free hours there, often the evenings, because that was the time when most of his customers were free to come. His stock was of necessity very small, but he soon saw that there was also a market for religious cards and crucifixes and rosary beads. His supply of books grew and he planned someday to do a little publishing of his own as did many booksellers of the day. He carried on his shelves *The Practise of Christian Perfection,* a popular abridgment of an old classic; Pastorini's *History of the Church* issued by Bernard Dornin; Taylor's *Book of Prayer,* and *The Chris-*

tian's Guide to Heaven. He had Bibles and copies of *Free-man's Journal* and the *Catholic Almanac,* pictures of prelates and saints and Father Mathew Temperance Cards, these last especially popular since Father Mathew had not long before lectured at St. Mary's.

It was a tiny shop among New York's booksellers—Kenedy's and Sadlier's and Ryan's and the others—but he was not trying to vie with them. Nor did he make a great deal of money from his shop, for no one in the parish was rich, but he did realize, along with his sexton's pay, enough to set aside a sum for his mother's future needs and for his expenses at St. John's. There, during the next few years, he attended classes when he could; and when he could not come to class, one of the professors was good enough to tutor him. For he interested the men who taught him, this man past his first youth, so eager to learn, so willing to work hard, and for one reason only—that he might someday be a priest.

He enjoyed the trip on the train to the college at Rose Hill. It was only eleven miles from the New York station, but the train traveled slowly and once outside the city the country was lovely. The time spent on this journey seemed like a brief vacation to him, away from the dust and ashes, the furnace firing and the sweeping at St. Mary's, and the long evenings in the bookstore.

St. John's College at Rose Hill had been started some years before by Bishop Hughes, and Father John McCloskey was appointed as its president. When Father McCloskey was named Bishop of Albany in 1844 Father James Roosevelt Bayley had succeeded him. Only a few students attended the college at first, all studying for the priesthood, though it was intended as a college for secular studies as well. In 1846 Bishop Hughes invited the Jesuits to take charge, and later they bought the property for their own use, and it became Fordham University.

Eventually the trip to Rose Hill proved too expensive for John's resources and also took too much of his time, so he went instead for instruction to the new St. Francis Xavier's College which the Jesuits had opened in New York on East Fifteenth Street. When John came to study there he found the school situated in an unbuilt area but near a few fine houses and farms. Since the neighborhood where he lived was very crowded with tenements it was pleasant to go for a few hours several times a week to Fifteenth Street; although it was not so green and lovely as Rose Hill it was a pleasant change from Grand Street. Then, too, each time he went John had the joy of knowing that every hour of class brought him closer to gaining the credits that would enable him to go to the seminary.

So the years passed. Always the hard work of a sexton, the grinding hours of study, the hurried trips to the school, where the Jesuits were so willing to help this student who could appear infrequently but whose intention was so large, the evenings in the little shop, and always time for the boys' club in the church basement.

Though each year that went by added more to the sum he needed for the seminary and to the fund for his mother, he was well aware that he was still a distance from his goal. The 1860s came, and by that time his mother's hair was white and she was an old woman. There were times, discouraged hours, when he felt as old as she. But when even his hope sometimes grew weak, it was she who encouraged him to persevere. He tried, however, to say as little to her on the subject as possible, for he knew that she felt he would have been a priest long ago had it not been for her. And she knew that John regarded the responsibility of her care as a compelling duty and one which nothing would make him give up.

Sometimes he went uptown to get away from the city for a few hours, to the section now called Fifth Avenue, where in 1858 had been laid the cornerstone of a new St. Patrick's Cathedral. Little building had been done, for the Civil War's beginning had stopped it; men and money were both needed elsewhere. But during the interval an American flag flew all day over the half-built walls. *Freeman's Journal,* John read, disapproved and declared "flags from spires will soon mean harangues from pulpits." But Bishop Hughes had sanctioned this display of the flag, and each time John walked by, he rejoiced to see the Stars and Stripes protecting the half-built house of God.

In 1864 John learned, when he came to his sexton's task early one morning, that Archbishop John Hughes was dead.

The next day the Archbishop's body lay in state in the old Cathedral, clad in his prelate's robes, his miter and crozier beside him, on the very spot where young John Drumgoole had seen him kneeling when he had been consecrated by Bishop Dubois many years before. John knew that Archbishop Hughes, like himself, had come to America as a poor Irish immigrant boy, that he had worked for a number of years as a gardener before he had the opportunity to study for the priesthood, and he drew inspiration and encouragement from the thought of the achievements of a man who had done so much for his Church and for his country. In those days, when anti-Catholic bigotry was rampant, the Archbishop had many times averted trouble by his wise advice to his own people and by his fearless and determined attitude during the "Know-Nothing" and other disturbances. Because of his stanch character and intense patriotism, he had won the respect and admiration of his opponents and the friendship of many distinguished American statesmen. Only the summer before, although he had been broken in health—so ill that he had to sit in a chair while he spoke to the crowds from the balcony of his residence—he had, at the request of Governor Seymour of New York, made an effort to put an end to the terrible draft riots that were raging in the city. And his words had done much to quell the bloody tumult that had lasted for four days, a time when looting was general and all business had been brought to a standstill.

John Drumgoole attended the Archbishop's funeral, a very imposing ceremony in which eight bishops and 200 priests took part. The city courts were closed that day as a mark of respect, and members of the state legislature as well as the federal government expressed their grief at the prelate's passing.

One day in the same year John came wearily home from St. Francis Xavier's, pondering on how hard it was to be among young men and to know his own youth gone forever, that each year that passed meant one less to serve God as he yearned to do. But this day his mother met him at the door in a state of great excitement. Her eyes, still warmly blue in her wrinkled face, were smiling and filled with delight.

"John," she all but threw the words at him, and spoke so fast he could hardly understand her. "John, you can go. You can go to the seminary. It will be all right. Mrs. Kerrigan came in this morning with a fine plan. She and her Michael want me to come to live with them while you are away."

He looked at her keenly. This sort of plan had been discussed before and always something had gone wrong. "Are you sure you would be happy there?" he asked doubtfully.

"Yes, John, very happy, and I can help in their home. I'm not an invalid, you know, and I've kept house for you right along. Annie will be good to me, you know that. And I'll be right next door to St. Mary's and praying for you to become a priest at last. Please be happy, John, for both of us."

There was no doubt that she spoke sincerely. The Kerrigans were good people, the salt of the earth, and he could safely trust his mother to them. He felt a load slip from his heart. And when Mrs. Kerrigan came and discussed arrangements, he knew this was right. This was the will of God, helping him.

Now matters moved swiftly to a climax. It had been decided that he would apply to the Seminary of Our Lady of Angels at Suspension Bridge, New York, to be received there as a student for the priesthood. The hard days at St. John's, the weary hours of study at St. Francis Xavier's, were going to pay off.

He learned he had been accepted at the seminary. Money would still be a problem, but he had saved for his mother's expenses and thought he could manage for his own. This time he felt his course would run to its appointed end.

He was invited, a few days before he was to leave, to come one evening to the Kerrigan home on Attorney Street right next to St. Mary's rectory, where his mother was already installed. He knew the fondness of the Irish for a farewell party and was not surprised when he found a goodly number of St. Mary's parishioners present.

They were all sitting around drinking hot tea and eating buns. The windows were opened wide, for it was a pleasant evening in September and the sound of children playing came to him from the streets. And now, for the first time, he realized that he must leave these children whom he had known and to whom he had taught not only how to play games but the love of God. He promised himself that when he was ordained he would come back here and help them again, for he could not imagine a life of work in which children had no part.

Suddenly he realized that someone was getting ready to make a speech, as Mr. Kerrigan was making a space in the center of the room and William Dougherty, one of the church trustees, was rising and clearing his throat. John assumed that this must be the prelude to a farewell speech to make the party complete. But he was not prepared for the content of that speech which, moreover, Mr. Dougherty was actually getting ready to read. A formal speech from one who could talk so readily and fluently was surprising.

He now addressed John directly. "Esteemed friend," he began, "I speak for a committee sanctioned by the approval of our beloved pastor and representing a portion of your numerous friends in the parish of the venerated old St. Mary's Church. Your going away affects us more than words can describe or action portray. Your friendly advice, the cheerful greeting, and the brotherly sympathy remain graven in our hearts. The glorious monuments of Catholic progress that have arisen in our day under the blessing of Almighty God and the invocation of our Patroness, while fostered by our venerated pastors, owe no small measure of their success to your unremitting zeal."

He stopped for breath, and around him heard the murmur of approval of his words. "Representing the laity of the parish in their share of the work," he went on, "we bear testimony to the fact that in carrying out the worldly efforts which God allots us to perform, toward the work designed for His services, *you* directed us in council and led us in action and we return thanks to God for the blessing He has bestowed on our work and we pray Him to pour His choicest blessings upon you and that His spirit may aid you in perfecting yourself to minister at His altar."

He was holding a small package in his hands. "As a trifling token of regard from your friends in the parish we beg you to accept from us not a silver trumpet nor even an elegantly mounted revolver nor yet a pair of spurs, but a trifling number of the greenbacked monsters that at present overspread and some say afflict our country, hoping that in your possession and under your control the said greenbacks will be restrained from doing evil and perhaps even become the means of doing good. Wishing you long-continued health and happiness and success in your holy desires, we bid our late sexton but our always friend, farewell."

For a few minutes John could say nothing at all in reply. He looked around at the smiling faces of the men and women he had known for so long and for whom he felt such affection. Outside, the voices of the children seemed to echo the words just spoken. He looked at his mother and saw her smiling though there were tears in her eyes. His own voice was choked when he spoke:

"There is nothing to say to you, dear people, only that my vision of years will be made reality now. My one fear, that perhaps I could not earn enough money to continue to the end, is gone. You will make me a priest, God willing, and I shall come back and bless you someday."

Next morning he was on his way to fulfillment.

4

Seminary Years and Ordination

THE SEMINARY of Our Lady of Angels, at Suspension Bridge near Niagara Falls, to which John Drumgoole went in 1865, was quite a new institution, its foundations having been laid only nine years before by Bishop Lynch of Toronto. Its grounds lay but a short distance from the great falls, and the sound of their rushing waters was the first greeting John received when he left the train at the railroad station.

The president of the seminary was Father Robert Rice, of the Congregation of the Foreign Missions, who had himself built the present college. When John went there it was still unfinished and Father Rice's plans for a chapel were as yet only an architect's drawings on paper. But already the new seminary was staffed with excellent men, and its reputation, despite its few years, was very high.

John found in his classes several other candidates from the New York diocese, one of them, John Mullen, a nephew of Archbishop McCloskey. But they were all young men, while John was now close to forty-nine years old. At first he was greatly troubled about this disparity in age and wondered what the others were thinking when they saw his graying hair.

He need not have worried. He met with nothing but

fellowship and friendliness from these young men. He was quickly made one of their company and soon found that his ideas were listened to with respect. As the months went by and he inevitably began to speak of his favorite topic, the subject nearest his heart—the neglected children of the metropolis—he met with an eager and interested response. All knew that this problem might well be their own someday and that what they could learn of his experience would aid them in their future work. John often talked of his boys in St. Mary's parish and in such a way that one day a student said smilingly, "But, John, you talk as if they were your own children. You are as proud of them as a father of his sons."

As he said this John began to smile, too, but he knew there was truth in the amused remark. They were his children, these youngsters of tenement and street, and he felt a personal pride in their pluck and their attempts to earn a living, to make their way among the people of an indifferent city. It was only when he thought of his mother or the boys of his clubs that he felt homesick for New York and the old life.

After a time his life became entirely that of the seminary. At first he was not happy, for when, at the beginning of his school year, he was confronted by the curriculum, he was startled to find how miserably little prepared he was to enter upon the studies necessary for the priesthood. The preliminary work he had done at St. John's and St. Francis Xavier's had been at best sketchy, for his attendance had been so intermittent and so limited by the necessity of earning his living. Then, too, his mind was essentially a practical one; he found he grasped facts more readily than he did principles and abstract thought. As for Latin, he had mastered only the rudiments. Now he found that many of the textbooks were in that language! For a time he was almost in despair.

But, as had happened to him several times before, just when he felt himself entirely defeated in his aims, help came to him. Father John Landry, prefect of studies and professor of several courses at the seminary, saw in the middle-aged man a special vocation. After long discussions with Father Rice on the subject, Father Landry suggested that he himself give the new seminarian additional instruction outside the regular classes.

Patiently he drilled his pupil in the principles of theology and aided him in the difficult Latin. And it was Father Landry who, when the four years of the seminary were completed, was to recommend John Drumgoole for ordination.

Sometimes between his hours of study John went for walks close to the falls. They were a wonder of nature for which his boyhood in the crowded streets of New York had not prepared him. He had heard many times of them and had read about them, but he had not been able to visualize their actual magnificence, their wild beauty, their awe-inspiring height. The sound of their waters was always in the air, fainter near the college, but even there distantly to be heard.

One day, as he stood watching the foaming torrents, he thought of a description he had read in one of the books in his shop on Grand Street. Its title in English was *New Discoveries,* and it had been written by the explorer Father Hennepin, a Franciscan friar who had been La Salle's chaplain on the *Griffon,* the first ship to sail the Great Lakes. John was delighted now to find a copy of this book in the seminary library and to read again the account of the first white men ever to look upon the falls. Even through the stilted translation from the French there came the awe and wonder with which the pioneer priest had viewed this evidence of the power of God, this tumbling mass of waters, these rainbowed mists that hovered over them—"a sort of cloud that rises from the foam even at noonday and above the tallest firs."

John sometimes thought how Hennepin's "vast and prodigious cadence of waters" was like the rush of Christian charity—the many small gifts and prayers, the acts of individuals all helping to form the great flood of love. Far away, and very small, the little rivulets started, each unimportant in itself but contributing to make the vast whole. He prayed that his own part in the future would be to be as one of those rivulets which, joined by thousands of others, formed the great torrent that was the love of God.

Sometimes in his leisure hours he went with other students to the Indian village not far away, or to the church on the Lockport Road. At others he crossed to the Canadian side of the falls to visit the Convent of the Ladies of Loretto, a community connected with the Abbey of Our Lady of Loretto in Dublin and where the Sisters were in charge of an academy for girls.

The schoolgirls in their uniforms of blue had been surprised to learn that this gray-haired man who sometimes came to see the Sisters was only a seminarian, and so at first had been the Ladies of Loretto themselves. But he had a way of talking to them and telling them stories of New York and its history that held their attention, and the girls used to wish he would come oftener. To the Sisters he spoke sometimes of his future plans, of the neglected city children, and of his boys' clubs at St. Mary's, and of those other boys he had not been able to help.

He had very little money, never enough to buy new

clothing, and the nuns, noticing occasional loose buttons
and rips in his worn coat, mended it for him and listened
to him while they sewed. He was so intent, so eager about
his future work that his enthusiasm sounded to them like
that of a boy. He made it clear to them that he felt his real
life was still before him and that it was youth he planned
to serve.

He told them of his plan for a home for homeless boys—
a place where they could study and play, perhaps a place
in the country where they could get some color in their
pale cheeks, a sunburn which they would never have in
the city streets. "And when I have the house," he said one
day, "I shall call it after the convent here. Its name will be
Loretto."

No one of those who listened to him doubted that his
dream would come true. He spoke so definitely and decisively that they could almost see the happy children playing in the green fields, studying in the airy rooms, in the
house built by his love and his belief that this was what
God had meant him to do. Like him, the Sisters had full
faith in Providence. To some his plans might have seemed
Utopian daydreams; to the Sisters, as to John Drumgoole,
they were very practical projects that needed only the
blessing of God to make them succeed.

While John was a student at the seminary he had little
money for trips to and from New York, and during vacations he devoted his time to working for the parish priest
in a small town across the Canadian border. Here he was
useful to the pastor in many ways, and especially enjoyed
teaching catechism to the children.

Among those who helped with the decorations in this
church was a girl named Mary Wallace who seemed to
John always so absorbed and happy and devout when she

worked about the altar that one day he inquired if she had ever thought of entering a convent.

She looked at him in surprise. "How did you ever guess that?" she asked, and told him it was her dream but that she had never mentioned it to anyone.

"If you wish, I'll speak of you to the Sisters of an order that I know in Buffalo—the Sisters of St. Francis," he said. And that very evening he wrote to the superior there.

At last the years of study were over, or nearly so. On December 16, 1868, John Drumgoole and three other seminarians received the tonsure and minor orders, and three days later they were made sub-deacons. The seminary diary stated that the following spring, on St. Patrick's Day, John officiated as sub-deacon at a solemn High Mass in the college chapel. A month later the same record again listed: "Sub-deacon, Mr. Drumgoole."

On May 19 of that year those ready for ordination entered on a four-day retreat. And on Friday, May 21, the diaconate was conferred on the four men from New York. The next day, Saturday, May 22, they were ordained as priests by Bishop Stephen Ryan of Buffalo. The preacher on this occasion was Bishop Bernard McQuaid of Rochester, a noted orator always in demand for ordinations both because of his clear, persuasive voice and the excellence of his advice to those entering the duties of the priesthood.

For those now being ordained at the Seminary of Our Lady of Angels the Bishop's words held a great poignancy, for they were going out now to face that world; they had been trained to meet its needs but were as yet inexperienced in the demands that would be made on them. The logic of the great laws, the theological and moral precepts—these they knew well; now they must take these teachings out of the classrooms and apply them to the care of souls.

When the Bishop spoke of the work they could do for young men, and how religious training such as they had been educated to offer could bring out a child's good qualities and serve to guide aright the young heart, his words had a wider meaning to the fourth of the group than they had for the younger men listening to him.

John Drumgoole now knew, as the others did, the abstract laws and the theological precepts, but he also knew from his own past experience how true were the Bishop's words regarding their practical application. To him they carried added meaning, for the Bishop was saying, clearly and beautifully, what he had himself so often experienced, when he brought together groups of boys in the basement at St. Mary's Church, that a knowledge of the love of God brought out the fine qualities in a boy as mere material giving of charity could never do it, that to help and also to reform a boy of the streets the love of God must be taught him by men who were filled with that love of God who were able to see, in the forlorn and unattractive outcast, the image of Christ and His love for him.

For the first time in some years John Drumgoole had been giving concrete thought to his own immediate future. He knew he belonged to the New York diocese, but he had been anxious to know where in that diocese he would be sent. He hoped it would be to a large city where there were working boys and street boys to be cared for. To his joy he learned immediately after his ordination that the Archbishop was sending him to his own beloved parish. His first appointment was as an assistant at the Church of St. Mary on Grand Street in New York City.

Father Landry, the professor who had made his ordination possible, promised to follow him to New York, for he was to assist Father Drumgoole in his first Mass in his own church.

Despite his happiness the new priest was very sad at leaving Our Lady of Angels and his friends the Sisters of Loretto who had been so kind to him and had promised him their continual prayers for all his future work. He would miss particularly Father Rice who had encouraged him in his darkest days, when Latin and theology had seemed hurdles too high for leaping. And he would miss the eager young men who had never made him feel an outsider despite his years and his gray hair.

On the evening when Father Drumgoole left Our Lady of Angels, Father T. M. O'Donoghue of the faculty wrote in the seminary daybook: "In going away, as ever when he was here, his whole manner showed what real love he bore for Our Lady of the Angels and her faculty and her boys." And one of his professors spoke for them all when he said of the newly ordained priest, "He is indeed a holy, holy man."

There was little doubt but that John Drumgoole had made for himself a very special place in the hearts of professors and students, all of whom had helped him in some way and all of whom he had helped in his way, if only by the example of his patience and humility. He did not realize in the very slightest how great had been his own contribution to his seminary. He could not see what an example his own simplicity, his deep humility, had been for these young men among whom he had lived during these four years. He knew only that he was very grateful to them, and happy that he had known them.

Happiest of all he was to know that he was to return to

his own parish, to his own people, and especially to his own boys. As sexton he had been able to help these lads, to urge them to better things, to teach them faith and love. But the power he now bore he did not then have. Always at the critical moment he had had to turn them over to someone else.

Now the oils, the ancient, beautiful, powerful words of consecration which made him a priest of God, had given him authority as well as a loving and devoted heart.

5

New York's Children—The Newsboys' Home

JOHN DRUMGOOLE had come home again, to his city and his parish, to his mother and his friends. It was good to know that his work was here, and that he would again be a part of their lives.

He hastened to the rectory at St. Mary's to present himself to Father O'Reilly, the new pastor, for Father McCann had died while he was away. Then he went across the street to the Kerrigans' to see his mother, who awaited him with joy and pride in her eyes.

He found her greatly aged. Although it was evident that she had been surrounded by loving care while he was away, it was a sorrow to him to find how weak she had grown, how slowly she moved. But, despite the wrinkled face, the feeble walk, the blue eyes twinkled with their old brightness as she looked him over carefully.

"You've put on weight, son," she said, "and it becomes you. And"—as her eye lighted on a neat darn on his coat sleeve—"have you learned to do the fine mending up north along with the other studies?"

He laughed. "No, Mother, the Sisters did that for me. They saw to it that your John was as well mended as ever you kept me."

On Sunday, May 30, 1869, Father John Drumgoole said his first Mass. Father Landry, true to his promise, was beside him to act as master of ceremonies. The boys on the altar were strangers to the new assistant at St. Mary's, but afterward several young men whom he had trained as acolytes came up to speak with him. One was the son of Mr. Dougherty who had made the fine speech when he went away to the seminary.

In the front pew, her face one happy smile, his mother sat with the Kerrigans during the Mass. Old friends, their faces solemn and content, were there to receive his blessing.

He had thought he would be deeply excited when he first stood at the altar as a priest, the fulfillment at last of his hope of years. Instead, he felt only a deep and quiet joy, and he wanted to repeat over and over the words, "It is good to be here."

When, later, he showed Father Landry around the church and explained that he had been sexton there for many years, Father Landry said thoughtfully, "And now you won't be opening the doors of the church to people. You will be opening the doors of hearts to God."

He had been at his new work only a short time when he received happy news: Mary Wallace, who had decorated the altar at the little Canadian church near Niagara, wrote that she had been accepted by the Sisters of St. Francis. And she signed the letter with her new name in religion: Sister Mary Catherine.

The new assistant found there was plenty for him to do at St. Mary's. It was a far larger and busier parish than it had been four years ago. To help Father O'Reilly there were, in addition to himself, two assistants, Father Baxter and Father McEvoy, and they formed a congenial team.

Other things had changed in New York. There was now

a new way of traveling through the city—an elevated rail-road—though horsecars were still the chief mode of transit. The newer city dwellings were being built uptown, and the neighborhood of St. Mary's held even more poor people than formerly. St. Patrick's had burned to the ground in 1866, but the vestments and paintings—the old dim ones which John loved—had been saved, and the Blessed Sacrament had been removed to safety.

Plans to rebuild were immediately made and carried out, for though work on the new cathedral uptown was progressing, the old St. Patrick's on Mott Street remained very important in the Catholic life of the city. So it continued for some years to serve as New York's chief Catholic church and still proudly guarded the jeweled vestments which had been the gift of Pope Pius IX.

When Father Drumgoole went to visit the rebuilt edifice for the first time after his return from the seminary and stood looking out at the scene before him, he smiled, remembering the open spaces that had surrounded it in his childhood days and Mr. Idley's fox. Now all about him were buildings and tenements and narrow, crowded streets.

Since his days there as sexton St. Mary's had changed greatly. Two tall towers had been built above its front façade, and the newly frescoed interior gave a far brighter appearance than had the dim old church in which he had worked. There was a fine new organ and a new bell. It had changed, he thought as he glanced about, but it was still his spiritual home. Here he had been server. Here he had been sexton. He knew the church as a housekeeper knows the rooms of a house she has long tended with loving care.

But no matter what had changed, one thing was the same —the swarms of children in and about the school. There were many more of them now. St. Mary's school had 600 boys taught by the Christian Brothers and 750 girls in charge of the Sisters of Charity. However, these children had homes and parents, thought Father Drumgoole, even though many were poor.

His heart went out with sadness to the others—the ragged and homeless children whom he had aided in other days. Their condition was no better—if anything, it had grown worse. Despite the efforts of city and private charity, there was no lessening of their need or their numbers.

Alongside a poverty so deep that many depended for food on the refuse from the city dumps, there was a growing prosperity in the metropolis. By 1868 Wall Street was already famous as the great financial center of the nation; Broadway was a glittering façade of beauty and fashion; Fifth Avenue had an elegant line of residences and some fine churches. There were several miles of marble and free-stone buildings. But the city government was inefficient and often corrupt; unscrupulous politicians, chief among them the Tweed ring, were robbing the city of millions of dollars. And for the line of stately buildings there was the terrible contrast in the tenement sections—houses like huge boxes, a little light from windows at front and back, the middle rooms dark, the banisters damp and rotten, the stairs broken. In the Fourth Ward 290,000 people were packed within a square mile. It was a region where typhus and deadly fevers often took their toll and where tenements were crowded from basement to attic and some lived in subtidal cellars. Cattle on farms were better housed than were some of the citizens of New York.

At a time when such conditions prevailed it is not to be wondered that the children of the poor were among the sufferers. The Civil War as well as successive epidemics had left many orphans, and the tremendous growth of the population due to a new upsurge of immigration in the postwar years meant a corresponding increase in the problem of homeless and destitute children.

In 1868 Father Hecker wrote in *The Catholic World* that there were 40,000 homeless children in the city. Hundreds from four to fourteen were found drunk. Forty-six hundred boys and girls from ten to fifteen had been arrested for drunkenness and petty crimes. Groups of frightened little children were occasionally to be found sleeping in station houses, permitted to remain there by the police while they searched for some place to put them.

Despite the work of bishops, priests, and religious, and the few wealthy laymen of the city who aided them, the Catholic institutions of New York could take care of a distressingly small number of these children, a large proportion of whom were of the Faith. In 1869 the six Catholic orphan asylums in New York were caring for some twelve hundred children. In addition there was in Westchester County the Catholic Protectory, founded in 1862 by a group of Catholic laymen with the assistance of Archbishop Hughes and under the presidency of Levi Silliman Ives, an Episcopal minister who had some years previously become a Catholic. In 1869 the Protectory cared for some 420 boys and 137 girls. This institute would take, according to its charter, "the child in circumstances of want and suffering, exposure or neglect, or of beggary." It was crowded and overcrowded before it had been opened a month, and in its very first year, although they regretted the necessity, the managers were forced by lack of room to restrict admission to those committed by the courts and the Commissioners of Public Charity.

But there were many little homeless vagrants who went to no school, who had done no harm to society, who even

earned a living, though a small and precarious one, by selling papers or cleaning chimneys or blacking shoes. These
children could not be brought under any existing law; they
worked, even though they earned little. They were not
legally vagrants and so could not be sent to any of the institutions then existing. That meant that they had no place of
shelter save what they won for themselves from night to
night, and often this was only a packing box, or a disused
icebox, or porch steps, or a grille over a warm cellar. To be
assured shelter, children must be convicted of a minor
crime or found drunk. The others lived as they could.

In 1853 Charles Loring Brace, a Protestant minister of
the city, motivated entirely by his deep sympathy for these
unfortunate waifs, had founded the Children's Aid Society.
He had seen boys, sometimes a half dozen, as Father Drumgoole saw them not much later, sleeping under a stairway,
huddled together to keep warm, or, on a hot summer night,
asleep on some porch steps or in an areaway. Completely a
Christian, he felt these children ought to receive shelter
and religious training. When he talked to them he found
them very responsive to him.

"Bummin' is hard work in a big blow," said one, and he
bore this phrase in mind when he opened a lodginghouse
for boys who were working and had no fixed home. He
rented an old loft in Fulton Street and furnished it with
bunks for seventy-five boys. Those who came were of all
kinds—some sharpened by years of street life, some already
familiar with crime and vice, others merely friendless and
ignorant and young.

He offered a bed and supper to these boys—six cents for
a bed and four for supper, since they were considered in
some degree self-supporting. There were those, of course,

who came merely to make trouble, and even those who stayed were for a time wary, fearing a "Sunday-school trap."

Before long the Children's Aid Society, which Mr. Brace founded to make the work more stable, branched into wider fields. It planned industrial schools, Sunday meetings, reading rooms, and paid agents whose full task would be to undertake these various duties and also to find boys for the lodginghouse.

In all this good work there was one constantly recurring difficulty for the Catholic authorities. It was that, though Christian, the work was completely under Protestant auspices. Though nominally non-sectarian, it was almost too much to expect that there should not be some proselytizing since, to some workers in the Society, Catholicism was a superstition and a threat to the American way of life, and they felt it a duty to substitute in childish minds other and better things. Even so good a man as Brace himself felt this to some extent. Anxious to get rid of any lingering narrowness in the thinking of those who cared for poor children, his reaction from the harsh Puritan creed made him include in his fear all creeds, including the Catholic.

Nevertheless the talks he gave to his newsboys always had a religious and moral trend, though he made an effort for them not to sound like tracts. Bread before sermons, he said, and rightly, but often in this effort to meet the practical needs of the poor his workers disregarded the Catholic practices of many of those they were trying to help. Therefore Catholic welfare workers had sometimes to oppose certain measures taken by this organization. This was especially true when the work entered an unfortunate phase that Catholics were not alone to criticize. It was stated as the Society's conviction that "the best asylum for an outcast child is in a farmer's home, that there they would meet with far better conditions than in any institution"; and so "on application" hundreds of city waifs were sent to farms in the Middle West to private homes. No doubt the shortage of labor in the West was a factor in interesting many of the farmers in the older children who could be expected to work for them.

At first the children were individually placed, but this proved expensive, and those taken for the most part from infant and orphan asylums and also from parents unable or unwilling to care for them were sent in groups of twenty to forty to selected points in the West. Their train would stop at a station; there, or at a church or schoolhouse, people came to choose a child. Then the children, for better or worse, were gone from other jurisdiction.

Mr. Brace made an effort to meet the criticism of this method of child placement by attempting to have his agents visit each adopted child once a year—a plan which proved impossible to carry out. He even published a booklet showing pictures of children he had himself visited, and he told of their happy life, and how they could leave at any time they wished—a difficult thing, said objectors, in the case of a small child more than a thousand miles from home. But since there had been many really successful placements the work continued, and by 1865 some 10,000 children had been sent to Western homes.

Many of these children, perhaps the great majority, were Catholic; it was obvious that since many of them were placed with persons of other creeds, they would never know of their faith again except to hear it mocked or called superstition. Sometimes letters came, years later, to the diocese, from children sent away when small and now grown up, asking for information about their parents.

Some worked their way back from the farms to which they had been sent. Once three ill-clad boys appeared together at the office of the mayor of New York, having come all the way from Kansas where they had been overworked and underfed on the farms to which they had been sent. Ragged and thin, they had been befriended by freight-car men on the long way home.

Once in Wisconsin a priest found a "sale" of children going on in a Methodist church. Discovering that nine of the twelve children were Catholic, he wrote back to New York, "It is my opinion that a terrible responsibility rests at the door of you New Yorkers whose duty it is to watch over these lambs of God."

This alarm had spread far beyond the bounds of New York State, and beyond the state authorities or the religious leaders of New York.

"Day after day," stated the pastoral letter of the second Plenary Council of Baltimore in 1866, "the unhappy children are transferred by hundreds to the sectarian reformatories where they have been placed, then to distant localities where they are brought up in ignorance of the religion in which they were baptized. The only remedy . . . is Catholic protectories . . . under the only influence known to have really reached the roots of vice."

And Dr. Ives, who had been for some years in charge of the Catholic Protectory in New York, said that whatever the state might or might not do, the duty of Catholics was plain.

John Drumgoole, the sexton, had often brooded over the vagrant child workers of the metropolis, and Father Drumgoole, the assistant at St. Mary's, still did. More deeply than ever before did he realize how badly shelter was needed for these helpless waifs. They needed to learn to read and write, to be taught industrious habits, and, above all, to be trained for some good occupation and a decent moral future. In those first days after his return to St. Mary's, Father Drumgoole often thought of Bishop McQuaid's sermon at the seminary—of what he had said concerning the difficulties of a boy face to face with an unfriendly world when he was ignorant and deprived of the aid of those who should be his chief protectors.

With no training, with no one to watch over them— what happened to these boys when they grew up? He now knew what happened to some of them. One day a cynical printer asked him to look through the windows of a saloon where were gathered a dozen or so young men, obviously already intoxicated though it was not yet noon.

"These men used to be newsboys," said the printer. And Father Drumgoole knew without being told that some of these young men would surely find themselves in prison before long. Was this the only answer?

He learned that others were as interested as he in the plight of neglected Catholic working boys. Chief among these were the members of the St. Vincent de Paul Society in the city. Named for the man who had so loved the poor and especially the children of the poor, this society had two basic purposes: to give material aid to the needy, and to keep Catholics in, or return them to, the practice of their faith. Clearly among their tasks was to come to the aid of distressed children.

More and more alarmed about the homeless working boys, not only because of the material difficulties with which these children met, but because so many of them were Catholic children, the St. Vincent de Paul Conferences went more deeply into the matter of their relief.

Early in 1869 a committee was appointed to investigate the whole question, and to examine one solution which was being worked out in Brooklyn, where the Conference had rented a house, employed a superintendent and a housekeeper, and was lodging working boys. The boys paid ten cents a day toward their room and board; the Conference made up the deficit. The committee also paid a visit to the Children's Aid Society and its similar project on East Eighteenth Street in New York.

Father Starrs, Vicar General of the Archdiocese, was present at this meeting, as were representatives of the twenty Conferences in the city. The committee suggested that the Conferences begin their work by renting a building in the lower part of the city, where one hundred boys could be lodged. A superintendent, meals, the cost of fixing up the house, and the rental would, it was estimated, cost about $10,000 for the first year and much less after that.

A warehouse was therefore rented at 53 Warren Street for $2,500 a year. By June of 1870 repairs were finished. A member of one of the Conferences was named superintendent and the house was opened at the end of July.

St. Vincent's Home for Homeless Boys of All Occupations was an instant success. Boys flooded the place, more than the expected hundred, there was great enthusiasm about the new home, and the Vincentians were delighted. Then, as suddenly as it had met success, the project began to fail. The boys often did not come back after a few weeks; few new ones came. It soon became clear that the trouble was that the superintendent was not the man for a task which demanded more than overseeing the premises and providing meals. The Conferences added a house mother to the staff, but there was little improvement; the house was empty half the time, to the chagrin of those who had opened it with such high hopes. Could it be that paid workers had no real interest in the boys? Were they not in need of guidance as well as shelter? Was the success of the similar project of the Children's Aid Society due to the fact that it had had as founder a Protestant minister, a man who talked to his young charges about religion and tried to make them live moral lives? Was this what was lacking in the Vincentian scheme?

At the next general meeting of the Conferences one member suggested that perhaps one difficulty of the Home lay in the fact that there was no spiritual director connected with it. Thereupon a discussion arose regarding the appointment of a new superintendent who would be a priest, or at least of the advisability of securing the services of a chaplain.

James E. Dougherty, a member of St. Mary's Conference, rose. "The Archbishop tells me that Father John Drumgoole has offered his services for this work," he said. "I know him well, and know he has been fretting over this problem for years. He worked for quite a while among such boys as these when he was sexton of our church and is doing it there now." He then proceeded to tell briefly the story of Father Drumgoole and his deep interest in vagrant working boys.

Several members were dubious. They had met or at least heard of Father Drumgoole, and though they did not doubt his good intentions or his zeal, they thought he was so old in years and so new to the priesthood that he would prove of little value for such an exacting task. However, a committee was appointed to discuss the matter with him. At the next meeting they announced their enthusiasm regarding him and said that they had little doubt but that he could carry out the work. There was needed now only the permission of the Archbishop.

In 1871 full control of the Newsboys' Home had been vested in Father Drumgoole as resident chaplain, though the society would continue to pay the rent and other deficits. These expenses they hoped to raise in various ways, by lectures and fairs and, if more was needed, it would come from Conference collections.

The Archbishop had suggested that Father Drumgoole accept from him the offer of living quarters away from the lodginghouse, but he begged to be allowed to live there. "Your Grace, let me stay with the boys all the time," he asked. "When I was sexton at St. Mary's I often wished with all my heart that I could have them with me day and night as if I were really their father. If I don't make my home with them now and eat what they do and put up with their inconveniences, I won't have much influence with them. I'm afraid my work would not be half done."

The Archbishop was much intrigued by this man, so old in years, so able in plans and ideas, and certainly capable, if his past history at St. Mary's was proof, of coping with boys. Several people had gone to him to warn him of the inadvisability of appointing an elderly priest to manage unruly urchins who were tough products of the streets. They pointed out the difficulties of the other superintendent—and he had been a younger man.

The Archbishop knew the Conference plans, however, and thought them sensible and far-reaching. He looked now at the strong, kindly face of the man who had been for so many years on the road to the priesthood, who was evidently competent and able, and, most important of all, so obviously filled with love for children, any children, good or bad. He felt no hesitation about giving his permission. The man's faith, he thought as he looked at him, was as large as his charity and his charity was so evidently as large as his faith.

As for Father Drumgoole, he left the Archbishop's house with his hopes high, his heart as high. As he walked down the street in the September sunshine, he found himself looking at some of the boys he passed, and when he saw a newsboy or bootblack, he said to himself, "There's one for the Home."

In the rented house he found exactly the room he wanted for his own. It was small, but large enough for him. It contained a single iron bed, and an old desk that could also serve as table for his meals. There was no carpet, and he decided he did not need one. On the desk he placed his big rosary, worn from handling, and over the bed he hung his picture of St. Joseph.

He drew up a daily schedule for the boys. First there were to be prayers together; then Mass and a short sermon drawn from the Gospels. Many people, no doubt, would have suggested a different beginning and a slower approach, but with him the spiritual factors counted so greatly that he quite naturally put them first of all in his lodgers' day.

Not many boys remained in the Home when he came there, and no one had gone out to look for the boys to bring them back; nor had anyone ever gone out to search for new lodgers. Father Drumgoole did both. Those too shy to come he sought in the streets of the city—each to him was a lost lamb that he was bringing home.

Soon word went about that the lodginghouse was in new hands. The boys still there—about twenty-five when Father Drumgoole arrived—were evidently reassured after they met him, and they sent out word about the new chaplain at the Home. The number of those applying for lodging grew rapidly and before long the house at Warren

Street was too small to house them. Three floors of the loft next door were rented and fitted up at a cost of $4,000, the amount being contributed by Vincentians and friends interested in the work.

However, it was understood that the rent for this annex and the running expenses would in future be the responsibility of Father Drumgoole himself, and he was satisfied with this arrangement. The money he needed would come, of that he felt sure. But this certainty was not born of any sense of his own power. It was simply that he had already enlisted the aid of a powerful Patron.

From the beginning it was clear to him that the one who could help him was the one who had taken such care of his Foster Child. It was St. Joseph he made responsible for this work of the Home. It was St. Joseph to whom he appealed, with whom he talked of his work and his failures and his hopes, St. Joseph whom he thanked for his successes. He was the Saint to whom his prayers had always been directed; now he made him, so to speak, a partner in this new enterprise for feeding bodies and saving souls.

Day after day he talked with him. Someone gave him a little statue of St. Joseph and he placed it on the chair in his room. When he had need of help or advice, he sat on the bed facing him and talked with him. If strangers outside the door heard his voice inside they might well think he was talking to himself, but his own people knew better. He was discussing the future of his beloved Home with the Patron of homes. It was to him and to his advice that he listened, and it was to his support and that of Our Lady that Father Drumgoole, from the day he undertook his work, entrusted these children.

6

‑›››

The Work Expands

WITH THE MONEY given him by the St. Vincent de Paul Society to alter and fit up the new space at 55 Warren Street, Father Drumgoole arranged a division of the new quarters into several sections. He planned for a chapel which would hold 250 boys, a big classroom, a lecture room, a gymnasium, and sleeping cubicles. The feature which perhaps brought the greatest delight to his lodgers was the purchase of several hundred little lockers, one for each boy, each of whom had a key in his personal possession.

But more than the arrangements of the house were changed under the new director. According to his plan, this was to become much more than a temporary hostel for working boys. He wanted it to be their real home, and already he had decided that if the boys wished they could continue to live there until they were earning six dollars a week. After that they would be able to pay their way in a respectable roominghouse and would be "graduated" from the Home.

On his first evening at the lodginghouse he had given the boys a short talk, and he then asked if any of them who had some special talent would be willing to entertain the rest. Some of them pushed forward one boy. "Weaver's wonderful," they told him, and Weaver rendered a very creditable song and dance.

"The show people would certainly snap up Tommy Weaver if only the poor boy didn't have those dreadful sore eyes," he said to Mr. Dougherty who had dropped in to see him and stayed for the performance.

The visitor nodded. "So many of the street boys have them that I supposed there's nothing to do about it."

Father Drumgoole looked determined. "Well, we'll see if we can't do something about it. They must be caused by neglect or dirt, and we won't have either of those here. Maybe after a while I can get a doctor to give us a little of his time."

Before long Father Drumgoole had cured his boys of sore eyes, and by very simple means. He placed beside each boy's bed a washstand and basin, with a roller for towels and a little dish for soap that was to be used by no one else. Before long he had all but routed out what had been considered simply an ailment to be accepted by the poor.

When visitors came, he always showed them these arrangements and in one report to the Archbishop he wrote, "These washstands, though plain, give a cheerful appearance to the dormitories, and the boys are so careful in using them that seldom is a drop of water seen on the floor about the beds." He sounded exactly like a proud father whose children have very good manners.

From the very beginning one man who gave great and unstinted aid to Father Drumgoole was James Dougherty, the Vincentian who had first proposed him for the work. A few others came to help, but Mr. Dougherty, out of his own experience, warned the new director that it would be much simpler to raise money than it would be to find people willing to work as volunteers. "When someone is asked for such help," he said sadly, "they don't exactly leap with alacrity. I was able to round up four people to help you—conditionally. But so far I've found none who can be relied on from the word 'Go.' "

But Father Drumgoole had a way with him. He moved slowly in his requests to the Vincentians for help with funds and even more so in asking them to work with the boys. But he managed to persuade a few to come in the evenings to teach catechism. Although some were reluctant at first, expecting, no doubt, to find a crowd of obstinate and troublesome rascals, they found, instead, attentive and sharp listeners who showed appreciation and behaved well.

It impressed the visitors greatly to find these poor little newsboys and bootblacks, coming from despised groups, often better behaved than the children from their own circles. They were surprised to find that these boys had remembered the discussions during earlier lessons the next time they met and that they had in the meantime been thinking over the problems raised. The boys were encouraged to a certain freedom in their answers, and the evening talks were not confined to the catechetical questions but to an understanding of them and the application to their own lives.

Mr. Sullivan, one of the volunteer workers, was greatly surprised at this when he came the first time. "They've got good heads," he said admiringly after he had listened for a while. Later in the evening he displayed those talents that made him a visitor whose performances were clamored for at future meetings.

First, to the delight of his audience, he stood on his head, and for a very long time, while the boys shouted approval. "Learned it in the army," he told them when he was again upright. Then he sang a song while Tommy Weaver danced, and when the boys learned he could also play the cornet, he became one of the chief treasures of the Home. He would tell stories of his days in camp where he had been a captain in the Irish Brigade and used to announce the rosary and the Angelus with his cornet. He played it for the boys, and it was a moving thing to see how quietly and intently they listened. He told them about his soldiers, too, and of how he set up a fine to be paid every time one of them swore. And with this money they had bought a fine new cornet for their captain. "This very one," he said.

One evening an excellent baritone voice was heard coming from the lecture room, followed by vociferous applause which showed the singer had gone over well. It turned out to be old Mr. McGibney who had never sung in public before but who now became a stock entertainer for musical evenings at the Home.

One evening Father Drumgoole distributed Miraculous Medals to the boys. The next day a bootblack came to him with his medal. "I showed it to a customer," he said, "and he asked me what I was carrying that around for. I didn't know. What is it for?"

There had been no time the night before to explain the medal and now Father Drumgoole sought a practical explanation for the boy and his customer. He noticed a lad near by sewing a badge on a baseball cap. "You know how fellows wear badges when they belong to a club?" he asked.

"Sure, my brother used to wear one when he went out with his team."

"Well, why did he wear it?"

"To show what team he belonged to."

"Well, that's why you wear this medal."

There was a little silence, then the boy's face brightened.

"Oh, I get it," he said. "We belong to Jesus' club. I'll tell my customer."

After he had been in charge for only a few weeks Father Drumgoole opened evening classes in reading and writing and arithmetic for his boys, and when no one else was at hand to teach them he did it himself. For he wanted these ignorant children to have some start toward an education, since it was the only way they could get good jobs in the future. He soon had several hundred books in the lecture room, and a dramatic club was started for the more ambitious among them.

Soon Father Drumgoole's help was asked not alone for newsboys. Grownups in distress came to him for food and he gave it, as much as his limited means allowed. From the beginning he had resolved never to turn away anyone who asked for aid, but it was growing clear that the work he had undertaken was not simple.

Once a reporter came to get a story about this new form of charity for newsboys. "Where do they come from?" he asked as he watched the long line of boys file into the dining room.

The priest shook his head. "No one really knows," he said. "They fall out of the clouds."

Father Drumgoole knew it did not really matter where they came from; what mattered was where they were going. And at least he knew that these slept warmly and ate well and could go to school in the evenings.

"Kin I get in?" asked a late-comer anxiously of a regular boarder in the Home. "Tim says it's full, and I don't have the five cents anyway."

"Oh, come along," the other boy said reassuringly. "He'll hang you up somewhere."

And he did, on benches if no beds were left. Colored children, at first timid and afraid of their welcome, were coming in now, brought in by white boys who were their friends. Father Drumgoole welcomed them all.

More and more the newsboys' lodginghouse was becoming a home, and Father Drumgoole was in every sense a father to the boys. He taught them cleanliness. He looked after their food and saw they wore fresh shirts at Mass on Sundays.

The boys felt independent because they paid their way—twenty cents a day for meals and lodging. This did not cover their expenses but it gave them the feeling that this was their home and they had a right to be there. But only on working days did they pay; on Sundays and holidays there was no charge. One reason for this was that Father Drumgoole wanted to be sure that they were with him for Mass. On Sundays there was beefsteak for breakfast, and it was also the morning selected for distributing new clothing to recent arrivals. Father Drumgoole provided each boy with an extra shirt to be worn only on Sundays and it was washed weekly and placed in the boy's own locker for safekeeping.

When he was given a big stack of religious pictures, he showed the boys how to frame them in black tape and each chose his own to hang over his cot. Often these pictures furnished the subject for Father Drumgoole's short talks. Always, along with the spiritual, he looked well after the material. In fact, in those early days he was parent, nurse, mentor, playmate, and provider for the boys who came to stay with him.

One evening in the spring after Father Drumgoole had taken charge as resident chaplain, the boys decided to give an entertainment in his honor. There were recitations and music and Mr. McGibney sang as a finale "Home, Sweet Home" to the accompaniment of Mr. Sullivan's cornet. "Barbarous measure, but with Christian feeling and a fair voice," Mr. Dougherty reported charitably in his diary that night. He loved music and no doubt had suffered, but the boys and the performers and Father Drumgoole, who had no musical ear, had all thought it fine.

On another evening when Mr. McGibney danced a jig to the delight of the boys, and some of them gave a minstrel show with an especially good "Bones," it happened that an incident occurred to mar the rest of the evening's perform-ance. When one small performer got stage fright and forgot what he was to say and do, some of the audience began to snicker. At this Father Drumgoole got up from his seat. "If the son is unable to continue," he said firmly, "then the father must go to his help," and he began an im-promptu speech.

Usually audiences at these affairs were very appreciative. They sat quietly and listened politely. "I only wish," sighed a volunteer helper one evening, "that society mem-bers were as polite."

Christmas at the Home that first year was something to remember. More than 300 children assembled for Mass and almost 200 made their Communions. Father Drumgoole's sermon was on blessings—creation, birth, baptism, the home that sheltered them, the Sacrament they were about to receive. At the end of Mass the recently formed choir sang the "Adeste Fidelis."

The dinner was donated by a member of the Leavy family, and it was a royal repast. Turkey and cranberries, mashed potatoes and stuffing, pie and ice cream—there was enough for everyone. And besides the boys more than a hundred poor people were fed, some of whom brought their children with them. These looked, thought Father Drumgoole in distress, not half so well fed or well dressed as his own big family.

Mr. Dougherty was here and there and everywhere, helping and giving orders at the same time. Someone came up to him and whispered that there was no extra supply of cups. "No cups?" he said in disbelief. It was only too true; someone had forgotten to order any.

An hour later Father Drumgoole found Mr. Dougherty sitting wearily in a chair. "I missed you. Where have you been?"

Mr. Dougherty explained. "There were no cups. I knew of a place on Spring Street that had extra stuff to rent so I got them and then ran back here and now I'm sitting down for a moment until"—he consulted his watch—"I go home for my own dinner."

During the day many people came to visit the Home, and Father Drumgoole was very proud of his polite and well-behaved children. It was with true happiness that he had seen them sitting together at his tables—the employed boys and the unemployed, newsboys, errand boys, apprentices, sweeps, all with no distinction of creed or color. The sheltering arms of St. Joseph's agent on earth were wide enough to hold them all.

On the eve of the feast an interesting thing happened. Father Drumgoole had decided to give a day's retreat for the boys, and they all had been willing to come to the chapel in the morning and the evening, but the idea of going to confession was a very different matter. Father Drumgoole learned accidentally that the older boys were planning to rush out as soon as supper was over, so he stationed himself at the foot of the stairs. When the ring-leader in the group came hurrying along, pulling his cap from his pocket, he stopped him.

"How fine to see you so eager to make your confession and give a good example to the little ones," he said blandly.

The boy, who was seventeen, and older than the others, was too surprised to lie or give any excuse, and Father Drumgoole drew his reluctant captive to the confessional. Afterward he congratulated the young man on his courage, and to his surprise the youth broke into tears. When he could control himself he told a hitherto-unrevealed story. He had run away from home after a violent quarrel with his father, a well-to-do businessman in a town some distance from the city. The basis of the quarrel had been the son's refusal to go to church, and especially to go to confession. Finally he left home, stole a ride on the trains, and two months before, penniless and hungry, he had been brought by a younger boy to the Home.

The other boys had been anxiously waiting for the end of their ringleader's interview with Father Drumgoole, as they were afraid to leave without him. When they saw him emerge, they rushed to him and asked what they were to do.

"Go make your confession," he said briefly, and later in the chapel Father Drumgoole gave thanks for this unexpected victory.

In August of 1871 the Vincentian Conferences heard a report on the results of the year's work at the Newsboys' Home. Lectures, boys' board, and donations had brought in about ten thousand dollars. Although most of it had been already spent, it was clear that the work was becoming well established as a charity that would draw support.

Moreover, in addition to the help from the Vincentians, the Home was now receiving aid from such organizations as the Irish Emigrant Society and had the promise of financial support from the city.

Mr. Dougherty suggested that for each Randalls Island child left with Father Drumgoole the Conferences pay five dollars a month. One member objected, saying that the rules would not permit this.

"Rules—rules—Father Drumgoole never made any terms with us," exploded the annoyed Mr. Dougherty. "Is it fair to start making terms with him? He takes every child sent him and says not a word about terms. The *need* is the important thing in a work of charity—not rules."

When the Conferences met again in January of the following year, Father Starrs made a proposal. "I suggest that we turn the Home over to Father Drumgoole, putting him in full charge there, but that we continue our financial assistance."

A committee was sent to discuss the matter with Father Drumgoole and a month later the change was effected. Now he became not only resident chaplain—up to this time his official title—but also superintendent and entire head of the Newsboys' Home on Warren Street. He had the promise of the Conferences, however, that their help would continue in some measure as long as there was need of it, and almost every man pledged to continue giving a hundred dollars a year as well as money to buy shoes for the boys. The Home would also receive a share of the proceeds from small lotteries at church fairs and sums received from lectures.

Father Drumgoole was well satisfied even though it meant a much greater responsibility for him. For now he was going to be not only spiritual father to his boys but

their material father as well. Eagerly and joyously he went
to the little chapel in the Home and put the whole matter
of the future of his boys in the hands of Our Lady who
was their mother and St. Joseph who was their protector.
There might be difficulties ahead and sorrow and loss, but
with such patrons how could one fail? A Child had been
their chief concern on earth. Surely they would watch over
these children who belonged to their Son.

At the beginning of 1873 the Newsboys' Home was becoming well known in the city, both as an interesting ex-
periment in the training of boys and as a shelter for the
homeless. Reports of its progress were sent by Father
Drumgoole both to the St. Vincent de Paul Conferences
and to Archbishop McCloskey. They were lucid and also
very brief, for Father John had little time to spend on fine
phrasing.

His report to the Archbishop began by stating that the
average attendance was 180 a night; because of increased
renting space he now had thirty-nine rooms and halls. He
had a hundred new beds with bedding and blankets, and
each small room was provided with a locker. There was a
new washroom and a powerful caloric engine which
pumped water to the upper floors and ran the washing
machines.

But in this report to the Archbishop he kept the best
for the last. He ended by saying that during the year 150
boys had made their First Communions and on the great
feasts, at Christmas and Easter, nearly all of them had
received Communion.

For reporters the Newsboys' Home made good copy, and
they never failed to leave without a human-interest story.

More than one of them was amazed when he saw the numbers of tough-looking boys running in and out of the house yelling affectionate greetings to Father Drumgoole. Their hands were black from shoe polish or newsprint or chimney soot. The younger ones swarmed around the smiling priest, pulling at his coat to get his attention, and the reporters noted that he called each boy by name. "Why are you coming in so early?" he would ask one. "You aren't sick, are you?"

"Feeding, washing, clothing, educating to the best of his ability and limited means," wrote one reporter of Father Drumgoole's tasks. In his own letters of appeal Father John was wont to say, "There is so much to be done for my boys and so little to do it with."

His helpers made up for their small number by their enthusiasm. Women who knew of his work met at the Home to repair clothing collected for the boys, and some made great loaves of bread daily for the Warren Street house. And Father Drumgoole could always count on someone supplying food or money or both for the parties to be given at the great feasts.

Eighteen seventy-three was a panic year, so terrible that it was on record that 900 people had actually starved to death. There were more than 11,000 homeless children in the city and more than 3,000 abandoned babies were picked up in that year, of whom a hundred were dead when found.

One of the saddest stories of that winter was told with sorrow by a night watchman. On his rounds he had seen a boy who seemed to be fast asleep in the shelter of a box of ashes, curled up with his tattered coat pulled tightly around him. The watchman felt sorry for the child and decided not to disturb him. When his night rounds were ended and he passed that way for the last time, he saw the boy still lying there and knew that this time he must rouse him or be considered remiss in his duty by his employers. The child paid no attention to the voice and when he shook his shoulder, to his horror the little boy rolled over stiffly; he was dead, having evidently died in the night. At the inquest the watchman explained, "I was but leaving him to his dreams."

During that cold winter every bed at the Newsboys' Home was occupied. In fact there were more boys than beds, and often the house was so crowded that boys slept on the benches rather than take a chance on spending the night in the street huddled over the heat register of a building. Even the warmth that came up from these grilles often had to be shared; one boy would walk about trying to keep warm while another occupied the grille for his allotted time of sleep. It was much better to spend the night on a bench in Father Drumgoole's dining room or on the carpet in the parlor.

On weekday mornings the boys left the Home to go to work or at least to try to find some employment; at five in the afternoon they returned. But of course that rule, like all the rules, was stretched during that hard winter, and a daily average of more than a hundred boys came home at noon for dinner.

Employment was scanty and the fifteen or twenty cents a day stipulated for food and lodging often went unpaid. More than seventy little boys were all that winter given food and shelter free. As for grown people, Father Drumgoole could still boast that no worthy applicant for food or shelter had been turned away. The books showed that this was no small matter, for thousands of meals had been given free. On Sundays outsiders were always present for dinner, and Father Drumgoole, knowing that sometimes some guest might be in desperate need, kept change in his pockets for such emergencies.

This year proved a very difficult one for the Home. A debt had been incurred when the second house was rented and furnished. It was for only $2,000, but, with the depression and consequent poor receipts, it seemed all but impossible to pay it off. Friends came to Father Drumgoole's help with funds for day-by-day needs, but it was now clear to him that if he wished to pay what he owed or to expand his Home further he must have a firmer foundation than such day-by-day assistance. More than once that winter, with the little statue of St. Joseph in the chair before him, he held long and anxious consultation with his Patron.

As a matter of fact, Father Drumgoole was in many ways very fortunate during that hard year, at least that was how some would have put it. He simply said that Our Lady had been with him and that St. Joseph had been his chief aid. The loan with which he had paid off the season's worst expenses had been made with no interest asked, and a thousand dollars received from the Irish Emigrant Society was a wonderful help. The day after that check came Father Drumgoole told the boys they must all give thanks for the splendid gift which was made to them all, and at five in the morning of a very cold winter day 200 boys gathered in the chapel to ask Heaven to bless the Society and their families.

⇛⇛⇛⇛⇛⇛⇛⇛⇛⇛⇛⇛⇛⇛⇛⇛⇛⇛⇛⇛⇛⇛⇛⇛

7

Visitors to the Home

OF THE interested visitors who came often to the Newsboys' Home, having heard in various ways of this priest's
work and his unusual methods, were some who were interested in charitable methods and others officials of the
city welfare organizations. One of the latter, Mr. Letchworth of the State Board of Charities, called one day, saying that he wanted to include something about this Home
in his annual report.

He was shown through the house and also through the
annex at 55 Warren Street. Father Drumgoole told him
sadly that already he was badly overcrowded but had no
money to provide further space. The visitor inspected
everything—the dormitories with double tiers of iron
beds, the coarse clean sheets and blankets, the dining room
where 200 boys were fed.

When he asked what food was provided for them, Father
Drumgoole said: "For breakfast bread and butter and
coffee, as much as they want. At dinner we give a full
meal, but we have fewer boys since their work takes them
too far away from home to come here. For supper they
have molasses and bread and some little extra when we
have the money. Our food does not rival Delmonico's but
to some of these boys it is just that. And the price is a
great argument in our favor, too—breakfasts are five cents

and supper the same. Lodging is five cents and washing is free." And then he added, "Of course if they have no work, we give them the food and shelter free."

Mr. Letchworth noted that there was running water for washing of hands and faces and that the washroom held fifty basins and looking glasses as well as a long trough for washing feet at night. He went through the gymnasium and chapel and schoolroom, and Father Drumgoole told him that the boys were given the rudiments of an education.

"What am I to give in my report as the chief object of your work here?" he asked.

Father Drumgoole smiled. "A very simple one—the object of the Home is to care for children, to bring them up, and to do exactly what a father would do for his children—help them until they are old enough to help themselves, to cultivate self-reliance and industry, and aid the boy to take his place in the world as an honest and self-respecting man."

"You would take any boy here no matter what his reputation was for mischief—or worse?"

"Oh, of course. Some of the worst cases—they called them 'terrors of the city'—have been here and now they are holding good jobs and would not go back to their old lives for anything. Of course with Catholic children the Sacraments have a great effect, but I will gladly take in children of any faith and color."

"You are more hopeful than some I have talked with."

"Oh, it's just that I look at it in a different way," said Father Drumgoole seriously. "I think it is really our fault that these boys are not better. Their condition is due to our neglect. The younger boys who are here are easy to control. They leave their bad habits with little trouble.

All they want are kind words and kind acts. Have you time to let me talk to you about one older boy?" he asked. When Mr. Letchworth said he had, the two men went back to Father Drumgoole's own simple quarters.

"One day one of my older boys met another on the street who was known all through the neighborhood as a 'hard case,' " began the priest. "My boy knew that I urge those in the Home to tell homeless ones to come here, and so this one said the other boy ought to come to see Father Drumgoole. The big boy laughed. 'He won't even let me in.' 'Sure he will,' the other insisted. 'He wants that kind—he says he's their chaplain.' So the big boy finally came in and said to me in a very bold way and as if daring me to help him, 'Here you are with a really hard case, mister.' But when I had him alone he dropped the swagger he had used with the boys. He looked very young and defenseless and he said, but sort of worried now, 'If you really like hard cases, you'll like me.' He certainly was one, too. He had been a juvenile Fagin with about twenty boys under him training to be pickpockets. He was scared now, for he knew the police were on to him. That was a few years ago, and now he has a nice job and wouldn't go back to the old life for anything. Pride—that's all—I gave him pride in himself. He has a bank account now. You see we teach them to save here, and we have about twenty boys with small accounts," he ended proudly.

He looked at Mr. Letchworth as if afraid that perhaps he was not making his point emphatically enough. "You would be surprised, Mr. Letchworth," he went on earnestly, "how easy it is if you go at it the right way. One little boy who came to live here told me that after he had been here a while he was down by the market and saw a purse sticking out of a man's pocket and was sneaking up to steal it when he remembered what I told them on Sunday about stealing—'so I didn't take it.' That is the sort of thing I mean."

Mr. Letchworth had stayed longer than he had intended, but Father Drumgoole had that effect on people. His reasons and his results, as one reporter said, were so refreshingly different. "You are doing a fine job here, Father," said Mr. Letchworth when he left. "I shall have a very good report to send about this Home. You are making what we need most of all—good citizens."

Father Drumgoole shook away the compliment to himself but this time, feeling Mr. Letchworth might not understand, he did not mention the great part St. Joseph had in the success of the Home. "That's one thing I tell my boys: they are American citizens," he said simply, "and I tell them that if they are faithful to God they will be faithful to their country, too. For I know that little can be done for these boys unless positive religious convictions are implanted in their minds—not too much religion, mind you —you have to give it to children in small doses, in five-minute talks and short morning and evening prayers."

Mr. Letchworth, like Father Drumgoole, knew well how much there was to be done for the children of the city and how hard it was to find the funds. "I hope you can keep on," he said. "While there is a single boy left to grow up in neglect in the streets of New York, it is neither in the interest of the municipal authorities nor her merchant princes to spare money or means to give him proper training or, if necessary, reformation."

"If I only had the means," said Father Drumgoole longingly, "I wouldn't be afraid to turn out one thousand reformed boys every year. And I have another idea that I want to carry out as soon as I have enough money and some more space. There are many poor widows with small children on their hands, and they must go out to support them. The children run about all day and of course they get into trouble when the mother goes out at seven in the morning and doesn't come home till evening. I want to have them stay here until she can come for them—and perhaps have Sisters in charge. In that way I could bring up a superior class of children. All I need is more room and more money. There are plenty of children."

Mr. Letchworth made a very fine report on his extensive visit, saying it had made a great impression on him to see the amount of good being done at the Newsboys' Home. "It is to be hoped," he ended his report, "that this worthy laborer in the Master's vineyard will soon have better facilities to widen the scope of the institution under his charge."

Another visitor appeared one morning in February of 1875; he said he was from England and gave his name as Rosebery; he was president of the Social Science Congress of Glasgow and interested in work for neglected children. The name meant nothing to Father Drumgoole, who received him where he received all visitors, in his little room with the single chair. There he sat on the bed and his visitor on the chair, from which he first removed St. Joseph with whom he had been discussing important matters.

The young Englishman was greatly impressed by what he saw at the Home—the clean little cubicles, the power machines, the little chapel, and the long list of those who had received help during the year. He said he liked the way each boy was given a private locker to which he alone had the key, the other ways in which the importance of the individual was considered. He said he had come to the Home because he had been intrigued by what a bootblack near the hotel where he was staying had told him about it. In England and Scotland he had been interested in the work of the Ragged Schools and wanted to know about this attempt being made in America to solve a difficult problem. Besides, he himself had been left an orphan at an early age and his interest in every orphan was deep.

The next week he came again, but this time his visit was more officially announced. One of the helpers came in with a dazed look on his face. "There's a lord to see you, Father," he said in awed tones.

Father Drumgoole was rather surprised at his assistant's manner, but concluded he had mentioned a Mr. Lord. When the caller came in he realized that this was his earlier visitor, and suddenly knew who he was, having seen in the papers mention of a Lord Rosebery, a man high in the councils of state in England.

They had a long discussion of the problems of the working boy, and then Lord Rosebery told him that in Edinburgh many of the indigent children were Catholic and, since he was himself a good churchman of his own faith, he had seen to it that they received an hour's instruction each day in the religion of their parents. "Had some trouble, too," he said. "There was opposition from those who thought that a Presbyterian country should not thus propagate error in an educational institution. But you can't let children be little pagans either."

Father Drumgoole said such objections were familiar to him, too. "Here every child is welcome whatever his creed. No matter what their faith they are all hungry and they all get cold."

Rosebery nodded. "I don't believe in the kind of charity which, if it meets two ragged children on the street, asks their religion, and if one says he is a Catholic and another a Protestant, says to the latter, 'Come home with me and take your porridge,' and to the other, 'As for you, little Catholic, you may die or starve or emigrate, it is no matter to me. I do not agree with any of the articles of your dogma and therefore you may be left to your own ways and doings.' "

Father Drumgoole nodded sadly. "We have such people here, too. There is one mission with the rule: If the place is crowded, Catholic children will be excluded."

As they left the room together, Lord Rosebery noticed a picture of St. Peter's in Rome on the wall. He stopped in front of it. "Ever been there?" he asked.

"No," said Father Drumgoole with regret. "My only sea voyage was when I came from Ireland as a little boy."

"You must go someday—and be sure to go to St. Peter's on a Sunday. There is nothing in the world like it on Sunday. I love to watch the congregation. What you see are not just glossy hats and fine clothes or a prosperous peasantry. You are elbowed by poverty, real poverty, but those people seem to realize that this church is really theirs. I saw them in rags and tatters praying with a passionate earnestness that showed the living reality of those services to them."

When they reached the subject of educating children, Father Drumgoole expatiated on his special interest—his night school held five nights each week. Boys who had not known one letter from the other when they first came were now able to read. Colored boys were among those who came, and he found them very intelligent. "The white boys brought in some of their colored friends and although they came very hesitantly they soon realized they were among friends. There are no color bars in this home."

Father Drumgoole showed Lord Rosebery a room which was his great pride—a room with a stage where entertainments were held.

"Now I see what you are doing," Lord Rosebery said smilingly. "You catch their souls in the chapel and with the play hall you entrap their bodies." And then he grew serious. "I do think one of the most important aspects of this work of yours is your emphasis on the importance of religion for these children."

Father Drumgoole smiled a little wryly. "It takes a lot of doing. After all, the first secular and godless school was founded a long time ago—right under the tree in the garden of Eden. This idea that you can educate the brain without the heart is what makes men of the Commune cry out for liberty and fraternity while they are destroying their neighbor's property without law or justice."

A few days later the Englishman came back once more. This time he was leading by the hand a ragged boy of ten. "I found him out in the street. No family, he said. No home. Name's Pat. I said you might take him."

Father Drumgoole did some rapid thinking. Of course there was no available cubicle. There never was, but he never turned a child away on that account. "Leave him with me," he said, smiling reassuringly at the boy who was evidently not sure whether to go or stay. "We'll find a place for him."

Lord Rosebery made plans for his protégé and left a sum of money to take care of him—"and for the others, too, of course, but do keep a special eye on Pat." The promise was made, though anyone around could have told him that Father Drumgoole's special eye was on every boy there.

Father Drumgoole thought he had seen the last of the interested Englishman but he returned once more, this time to talk about Pat's future, saying he had decided to make it his special care. As he was just in time for the evening's entertainment, he gravely paid his admission fee of five cents, the usual price to outsiders though the boys came free. He applauded vigorously the song-and-dance acts, and afterward gave a short talk which the boys cheered loudly in their turn.

In the late autumn of that year a list of donations received by the Home during the year was printed, and it was noted by someone that the name of the Vincentians appeared in smaller type than that of Lord Rosebery. "We do not work for human praise but we have our feelings," said one aggrieved Irishman at a Vincentian meeting.

The pacific Mr. Dougherty rose to quell a possible tempest. "He never meant to slight us. Aren't we all one family in the Lord anyway?" And from the rear came another voice to aid him. "And it's the French would call it an *entente cordiale,* eh? And aren't the Scotch and the English Christians, too?"

On a hot August day of 1874 Father Drumgoole received word that his mother had suddenly become very ill. He hastened to the house where she was living and found her in a state of complete collapse. One of the priests from St. Mary's had been there, he was told, and had anointed her. The doctor would return in a few minutes.

He went softly into the darkened room, its shades drawn against the hot sun. He bent over the bed, then, thinking she was asleep, he straightened and started to go out again. But she had heard him.

"Johnnie," she whispered, and tried to smile at him.

Though he was shocked at the change in her since he had seen her the week before, he found no change in the look she gave him—the same look of affection as when he was a small boy returning from play or when he was a young man coming home from work. She could speak only with great difficulty, and he bent close to hear her. "All your boys," she was saying. "I'll tell the Blessed Mother the good care you take of them."

He smiled. "And tell her, too, what good care you took of me." He doubted if she heard him say that, for the one effort to speak had evidently exhausted her. She closed her eyes again and her face was still and withdrawn.

When the doctor returned, he asked about her condition. Dr. Held shook his head. "She may go any hour—in fact, any minute," he said. "She has an illness for which there is no cure—old age."

Father Drumgoole went to sit by the bed. There was silence in the room; the sick woman's breathing was the only sound in the stillness. He sat looking at her and remembering his mother in her youth—her pretty hair, her lovely laugh, her constant loving care of him. How fortunate he had been. It was really only right that he, who had had such an affectionate and loving mother, should take care of children who had never known one like her.

While he was sitting thinking of long ago—of Mott Street and St. Patrick's of forty years past, he saw that his mother was stirring. He had promised to call the doctor from the other room if she became conscious, but he had no time to do it. She opened her eyes wide, but this time it was evident she did not see him. She was looking beyond him. He rose and bent over her, but even as he did so, the eyes closed again and one small sigh was her last breath.

He made the necessary arrangements for her burial in

Calvary Cemetery, and in the morning he said a Mass for her soul and asked the boys to pray for her. From her room he had taken only one thing—a picture of Our Lady and the Child which she had brought with her from Ireland and which had been with her ever since.

8

St. Joseph's Union and the Great Bazaar

ALTHOUGH the chief reason for the existence of Father Drumgoole's Home was to provide a refuge and care for working boys, he was faced with many other problems. The Vincentians and other men who worked with him, and who knew how easily he was moved by such sad cases, often brought younger children to him. At times he could arrange to have them taken in by an orphan asylum, at others by a private family. But there were times when the responsibility placed before him was his only, to take or to refuse.

In March of 1875 Mr. Dougherty brought a little boy and a girl to the Home. The mother, he told Father Drumgoole, was dying and she wanted the children brought up in their own faith. The father said the neighbors had told him of a very fine Protestant place which would take the children and a very nice lady had already come to arrange it, but he had also said that if the Vincentians found a home for his babies he would give them up to them.

So Mr. Dougherty had hurried to the lodginghouse and told his story and the need for immediate action. "The judge said he could commit the little boy to the Catholic Protectory if necessary, but the little girl is under two and her case is much more difficult. Even the boy is under seven, but the Protectory will make an exception in his case."

Father Drumgoole looked troubled. "I don't like court commitment for a boy who has done no wrong. It looks bad and might hurt his future. I'll take the little boy, and we'll persuade Sister Frances over at the Asylum to take the little girl."

And so a six-year-old became a member of the lodging-house where hitherto the boys were supposed to be self-supporting.

Not long afterward Patrick Nolan, a Vincentian, who worked at Randalls Island, brought Father Drumgoole a much more difficult problem. He had learned that a part of the Island was being closed, which meant that a considerable group of children, some very little, were without a place to go. Hiring a truck, he suddenly appeared at Warren Street with more than forty small children.

For perhaps the first time Father Drumgoole was nonplused as Patrick explained, "The Commissioner of Charities will take them only if the authorities promise eight dollars a month for each child and pay in advance. There is only the jail left. The asylums are too full for such a big crowd."

The children were huddled about Mr. Nolan, and some were crying, no doubt from alarm at being removed from the poor place that had at least been home to them. Father Drumgoole looked at them. The lodginghouse had no quarters for them unless a room could be fitted up as a dormitory and some of the women who were his volunteer helpers could increase the time they gave him. He did not hesitate long, not with that sad group before him. He could find the room; he knew the women would rally to him. So he bade Mr. Nolan bring the children in, and some he carried in himself. The heart, thought the relieved Patrick, expands to meet the need.

The next day the Vincentians arrived with promises of financial assistance to aid Father Drumgoole with this new group. The women volunteers on whom he had counted came to make over old clothes for the children and to help with their care during the day. Of course what he needed right now was the help of Sisters. But he knew the poor Sisters of Charity were already terribly overworked. And if he did get some other congregation to send him nuns, where would he house them? And where would he get the money for their support?

What he needed the most was some kind of definite income on which he could depend, rather than on spasmodic even if generous gifts. And more and more the Vincentians were withdrawing their direct aid, which was perfectly proper since his work should now be put on some firm financial footing.

He had thought of this often during the past year, and it was one day while he was in deep consultation with St. Joseph that an idea came to him. The plan conceived that evening in the quiet of the shabby little room at the Home was to have such far-reaching results that there can be no doubt that St. Joseph lent an especially attentive ear to the troubles of the priest who had enlisted him as his working Patron.

That evening Father Drumgoole came to a decision that affected the future course of his work. First, he would establish a union of contributors who would send him a small sum yearly for the work of the Home. Second, he would try by some means to raise one large sum as quickly as possible to provide immediately for his project.

It did not take him long to decide on a name for the

group of those who might answer his appeal. He would call it St. Joseph's Union. The members of the Union would share in Father Drumgoole's Masses, in the prayers of the children of the Home, and in the Masses said throughout the world by missionaries whose help he would enlist by sending them Mass stipends.

Of the best way to gain the interest of prospective members he was not certain until one morning early, as he was praying in the chapel and saw the boys come in, clean, rested after a night's sleep in a bed, knowing that they would be fed—and thinking of those others who had spent a night in the streets—it came to him that perhaps a little magazine would best let people know how needed and acceptable their small contributions would be—twenty-five cents a year for dues would be about right, he thought. And he would call the magazine by a phrase that was in his thoughts every day—*The Homeless Child.*

He determined not to wait long to put his scheme into operation. He needed so much and had so little. And he could not bear to see children literally grow up in the streets or on the dump or the docks, utterly illiterate, exposed to hardship and vice. At present his Home could take so few of these small victims of a harsh economic system. "It is not the will of your Father in heaven that one of these little ones should perish," Our Lord had said, and Father Drumgoole felt the responsibility of answering, as far as he could, that command.

First of all, he would go to see Cardinal McCloskey for advice and permission. In March of 1875 the Archbishop of New York had received the red hat of a prince of the Church—the first given in the United States. He welcomed Father Drumgoole with pleasure and listened to him attentively.

"I know well that new buildings do not come from wishing for them," Father Drumgoole told him. "And I need larger quarters for my boys, Your Eminence. I am so afraid that by fall there will not be any possible room for all who ask to come. Even with the use of the building next door, some boys had to sleep on benches and tables last winter. I could not turn them away," he added apologetically. "And now, in addition, I have about fifty young orphans in my Home—all under ten—and all entirely dependent on me."

He then outlined the plans for which he wanted permission, and the Cardinal listened intently to the priest who had become so late in life the shepherd of a flock of homeless little ones and who was so troubled about the lambs of his fold. To listen to the hopeful plans of one so well advanced in years and yet in spirit so young was an inspiration and a comfort.

When the Cardinal had heard all his caller had to say, he told him, "Do what you can and are able to do. You have my blessing on your efforts, and I hope to give you my substantial help as well." After the shabby priest had gone away happy, he said to himself, "And the hand of the Lord is with him."

Now, with the Cardinal's permission granted and with his blessing, Father Drumgoole got actively to work. He faced no small struggle: new property must be bought; new buildings must be erected. The question was how and with what? The Cardinal's encouragement was of the utmost importance, his own friends would rally round and help. But he must think of a plan for raising money at once and in a large sum. This money would have to come from many sources.

It was the ever-resourceful Mr. Dougherty who gave him

the best idea of all of how he might collect funds quickly.

"I hear they had a lottery at St. Teresa's last month and raised a lot of money. They had a fine list of names— 6,000 of them—and they'd give them to you to start with."

After thinking this over, Father Drumgoole went again to the Cardinal and, with the latter's approval, he prepared a circular about the lottery that explained his reasons for holding it. With the funds raised in this way, he wrote, he hoped to put up a large building—"where homeless and destitute children can enjoy all the advantages of a Christian family, learn their duty to God and neighbor, and in time take their places in society as honest and good men and law-abiding citizens."

This was his greatest need—more room for more boys. Room enough so there would be beds for every one of them, not just places on benches when all the beds were filled. On a few occasions there had been no room at all, and then he had to put blankets on the floor for the boys on bitter nights. He could not bear to think that some children, through no fault of their own and through lack of a decent shelter, were driven to find it in vicious places where they would become familiar with vice.

In addition he knew his night school must be enlarged, and this meant money for teachers as well as for more equipment, more rooms. Some children were coming to his night classes now who could afford to pay their own way in a boardinghouse but lacked the time for day schooling. He wanted to help them, too.

The buildings he had now were not only inadequate, but their rental was $4,000 a year, and if he had his own building he need not have this expense. Even with his present accommodations 10,000 children had already been sheltered at Warren Street; more than a thousand of them had been prepared for First Communion. And best of all, those he had placed in jobs were working well; employers had told him that his boys were honest, good workers— boys who had been guttersnipes when they first came to seek shelter at the Home.

Chief and foremost in his mind was the establishment of a building fund. Further than that he did not plan at this time. But one day when he was walking home and saw how dingy and dirty were the city streets, another long-ago dream came to his mind which he firmly suppressed for the time being. Someday, when St. Joseph and Our Lady had built the home for children in the city, perhaps a home in the country could be found, too, a place where the little ones could run and play to their hearts' content.

As for the city home he was going to build, he had the name for that even if he had as yet nothing more. With St. Joseph for patron, for whom else could he name it than for his partner in caring for the Child in the little Nazareth home? He would call it the Mission of the Immaculate Virgin.

On one thing, despite his urgent hopes, Father Drumgoole was firmly resolved: no building would be begun until he had all the money in hand necessary for its completion. There must be no debts, and so he must wait until the sum needed was collected. He knew the land alone would cost a large sum, and had been greatly alarmed when he learned the cost of city land in the neighborhood where he wanted to buy. Once, after pricing various properties, he had come home to his room and put St. Joseph into the old chair and talked with him seriously and long. That day when he emerged from his seclusion, several persons in the house spoke of the serene and happy expression on his face.

The original idea of the lottery was growing: it was

planned to hold a bazaar where the drawings would be made and the prizes given out. There would also be a concert. Since the affair soon gave every indication of being large, it was decided to hold it in Ferraro's Assembly Rooms on Fourteenth Street, next to the Academy of Music. The tickets were to cost twenty-five cents and with each ticket came a chance to win a prize in the lottery. As the months went by the prizes donated for the affair reached wonderful proportions. Some were sums of money; one friend contributed $300. There were a pony and cart, a washing machine, an Irish spinning jenny, a dinner set, a bedroom set, pictures of the Pope and the Cardinal, "the finest workbox in New York," silk hats, meerschaum pipes, General Sherman's *Memoirs, Lives of the Saints,* barrels of flour, and tons of coal. The winner of the spinning jenny would be taught how to use it "by a lady of seventy who will spin a hank of yarn for the winner."

Father Drumgoole had addressed the circular containing his appeal to all friends of the Home, to heads of families; members of sodalities; to schools; protective, benevolent, and temperance societies; Catholic literary associations; printing houses; stores; hotels; all of whom were urged to assist in this undertaking. All over the city tickets were sold—in bookstores, in offices, at the St. Vincent de Paul Conferences. An undertaker offered to take a block and so did a baker on Third Avenue. In Harlem there were several agents, and in Brooklyn, too. From Brooklyn, however, came the one refusal to help: Swayne's bookshop would not take any tickets because the owner objected to lotteries.

There was a suggestion that Manhattan College might allow its famous band to play at the bazaar. Father Drumgoole was hopeful but dubious: it seemed too much to ask.

But Mr. Dougherty offered to try, anyway. A few evenings later he came in triumph to the little office. "I got 'em," he announced triumphantly.

The year 1875 was almost over before the great bazaar was held on November 30. By that time it had been advertised everywhere, and tickets had been sold in almost every state in the Union. There was little doubt but that the wording of his advertisements had greatly helped Father Drumgoole. He had written most of them himself and in his own persuasive way. "On many occasions we are obliged to refuse children admission for want of room," ran one. "This means that thousands of well-disposed children through necessity, without any fault of theirs, are compelled to seek shelter in places where they are exposed to all sorts of temptations, imbibe vicious habits, grow up without any knowledge of the duties they owe to God and their fellow men, and are liable to become troublesome members of society."

Directly or indirectly he managed to interest a great many people in his project that year. Even before the bazaar money poured in. Many besides Catholics contributed, for the charity was becoming well known and highly approved.

Long before seven o'clock on the evening of the bazaar a great crowd began to gather. The disgruntled policemen on duty began to think the whole city was arriving en masse. It soon became evident to them that one of the biggest crowds New York had even seen was jamming into Ferraro's Rooms. But they knew that the huge edifice could accommodate as many as 10,000 people. Their pious hope was that no more than that would come.

But such a hope was not fulfilled, for, although the night

was very cold, at a little past seven o'clock the hall was overflowing, and so were the other rooms in the building, the corridors, the balconies filled with those who had come to hear the music and watch the drawing of the lottery. Despite the lack of comfortable seats, those who could not get inside showed no sign of departing.

At first Father Drumgoole and his helpers were afraid that someone would get hurt, but they were soon reassured. "I think I can safely say," Father Drumgoole said proudly as he looked over the orderly crowd, "that never before has a larger or more respectable assemblage of ladies and gentlemen met in this city."

Later estimates put the attendance at from 35,000 to 40,000 people. When the concert began, some of those present were able both to hear and see, but many had to be content with only hearing. Outside, it was close to zero; inside, the temperature rose to the eighties.

No accidents took place, however. The only near accident involved Brother Jasper and the Manhattan College Band. Washington Haggerty, sent to bring the band to the bazaar, had been so anxious that the stagecoach drivers do their best that he had warmed them up beforehand—with too much warmth evidently, for one ran the pole of his stage into a door. But Brother Jasper and the boys emerged from the coach unhurt and ready to play their best tunes.

The police present for the purpose of preserving order did their best to keep more people from coming into the hall than it could hold, but even after the music began crowds were still trying to press in and continued to arrive at the outer doors. The congestion in the streets outside was so great that the trolleycars on Fourteenth Street from Third to Fourth Avenues were forced to stop running for more than an hour.

The evening opened with a potpourri of Irish airs, which were vigorously applauded. Then Father Drumgoole came forward on the stage and was greeted with cheers. For a time the enthusiastic applause all but drowned out his efforts to speak. When he could make himself heard he expressed his thanks for the ovation and also for the generous financial response to his appeal. He then proceeded with a brief description of his Newsboys' Home and how it was run, giving figures to show the inadequacy of the present quarters at his disposal. He then spoke of his hope that now through the generous efforts of those present God would bless the work. The whole bazaar, he said, had for its one purpose to raise money for a new home for the boys, and it would be called the Mission of the Immaculate Virgin for the Protection of Homeless Children.

After more music came the distribution of prizes. To the front of the stage was brought a large drum in which all the lottery stubs had been placed. And the drawing was begun. It was well under way and twenty-eight winning numbers had been announced when a movement in the audience caused a growing murmur of surprise and also of annoyance. Police were seen forcing their way through the crowded aisles of the hall. The people present clearly resented this intrusion, and were slow to make way for the officers, but eventually Inspector Dilkes reached the stage and walked up to the astonished Father Drumgoole.

"I have been sent by the Police Commissioner to notify you that this drawing must be immediately discontinued. It is in violation of the law and I have orders to stop it."

Father Drumgoole greeted him quietly, but was obviously puzzled by the demand. "Of course the law must be observed," he said, "but it certainly seems to me that an earlier notification might have been sent me, Inspector.

You surely must realize what confusion this will cause in this huge audience."

"I do realize it, and it is too bad," said the inspector, "but I must perform my duty and follow orders given me to stop this drawing."

"Are you sure there is not some mistake?" asked the priest once again. "This is no lottery in the legal sense of the word. It is a concert and a distribution of prizes, and its whole object is charity—the raising of money to save children who have no home but the streets."

"I understand all the facts," said the inspector patiently. "I know of your work, of course, and I do not like to interfere. But I can only follow orders."

Father Drumgoole sadly faced the audience which had been watching with growing impatience the confusion on the stage and the colloquy between the two men. When he began to talk, the noise died down. He found it very hard to go on with what he had to say.

"Ladies and gentlemen," he began, "I have just received painful and unexpected intelligence from the Police Commissioner to the effect that this distribution of our prizes is illegal. Whether or not it is I cannot say, but the authorities have so decreed. It is therefore our duty to stop at once. Had I had the faintest intimation that this interruption would take place I would have made different arrangements, but I had no notification from the authorities or anybody else in regard to the matter and so it was impossible to foresee what has happened. The rest of the lottery numbers will be drawn elsewhere. The prizes will be distributed privately in the presence of the judges selected, and the numbers drawing prizes will be published in the newspapers."

From the audience rose cries of "Shame!" and "It's not

fair!" Some shouted that the drawings should go on a way, but Father Drumgoole shook his head at this demand. When it seemed there might be actual resistance to the officers, he appealed to the audience again. "There are hundreds of women and children in this vast crowd," he called to them, "and they are here under my protection. I would rather abandon the work forever than have any disturbance here or for blood to be spilled this evening."

The drum was removed from the stage amid a confused sound of hisses and shouts that could be heard over the music of the band which had hurriedly broken into an Irish air. When the people finally quieted down, the concert went on. But the harm had been done, and anger and resentment remained, for many present regarded the whole incident as an insult to a wonderful Catholic charity.

As people in the audience filed out discussing the affair they were immediately besieged by those outside the hall who had not heard of what went on within but had seen the officers enter and the drum being taken out. A truck had been hastily summoned and the prizes and the drum taken to Warren Street where the drawing was completed in time to put the results in the morning papers. Many in the crowd went along to watch.

For Mr. Dougherty and the rest of the Vincentians and the other helpers it had been a busy evening, but at last it was over. Father Drumgoole joined them, still annoyed at his treatment by the police but happy about the good behavior of the great crowd, and with the *Tribune* reporter who had come along for the story and Maurice Holohan of the *Catholic News,* went to French's Hotel for coffee and cakes. As they finally went their several ways Mr. Dougherty was heard to observe, "The one thing I still do at home —and the only thing—is to sleep there."

Some of the bazaar prizes had been won by people in distant parts of the country, even in the far West, and many in New York were among the winners. Among them were Bishop Corrigan, who won a ton of coal, and Monsignor Farley, who won the spinning jenny!

The programs had borne a note saying that Father Drumgoole would soon issue a small publication to be distributed free to all contributors to the bazaar and to those friends who had bought tickets. Sixty-two thousand tickets had been sold and their holders thus automatically became members of St. Joseph's Union and were entitled, among other privileges, to share in the benefit of two Masses each week for one year and to a copy of the new magazine, *The Homeless Child,* of which Father Drumgoole hoped to send them the first issue before many months had elapsed.

He was delighted with the fine financial returns from the bazaar. He was enabled to pay promptly a debt of $4,000 on the Home, and $10,000 was left to put in the building fund. "We shall not begin to build until the ground selected for that purpose is paid for," he wrote. "If members of the Union zealously labor for this cause it may be accomplished before the end of next year."

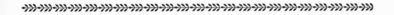

9

Growing Responsibilities—
The Homeless Child

ON THE Fourth of July 1876 the centennial of the nation
was observed with much éclat, and nowhere was it more
joyously celebrated than at the Newsboys' Home on Warren Street. The building was decorated with flags and banners that had been sent by a friend; George Washington's
picture in the dining room was draped in bunting. There
were recitations of a patriotic nature and a play was performed by the dramatic club.

When this was over Father Drumgoole came upon the
platform and said solemnly: "Now we are going to tell you
very briefly of a land made free." Then one of the older
boys read, very slowly and distinctly, the Declaration of
Independence. Afterward there was ice cream and cake and
the evening closed with a spirited rendition of the "Star-
Spangled Banner."

In that evening's audience there was a group of unexpected guests, the eldest among them perhaps eight years
old. That morning someone had asked to see Father Drumgoole in the parlor, and there he had found a troubled
gentleman and, huddled about him, six very dirty and un-
kempt children.

"My name is Sullivan, Father," he said, "and I am president of St. James' Conference. This morning a woman

brought these children to me and said she had collected them in the street where she found them sleeping. Between us we tried to find their parents. A few of them we did locate, but they were too drunk even to hear what we were saying, and the children cried when we took them home and were evidently afraid of their parents. We fed them and then thought maybe we could bring them here. Could you perhaps take them, Father, just for the time being?"

Father Drumgoole looked at them, and they stared back fearfully at him, some still crying. Smiling at them, he turned to Mr. Sullivan. "They come to us on a fine day," he said soberly. "Of course we shall take them."

Mr. Sullivan sighed with relief. "Then you have room for them, Father?"

Father Drumgoole shook his head. "No, we are full up, right to the last bed. But how can I turn them away?"

He called his helpers and the children were bathed and given breakfast. In the clothes room were found garments, too large but clean, for the newcomers. After a good scrubbing, the children were brought back to him, still timid and frightened, edging close to one another as if there, in a sort of sad little union, was their one strength. But he held out his arms and with one impulse they ran to him as if for shelter, holding to his legs and arms and to his old coat.

That night the little newcomers slept on cots begged from friends. When Father Drumgoole came in to look at them they were all sound asleep. As he blessed each one, he prayed with his whole heart that very soon his new Home would be built so that there would be room for little waifs like these with whom the city was strewn.

Other children were brought to him by friends or the police or even by strangers who had heard of his Home.

Sometimes they were found sleeping in the street or begging, or weeping in terror because a drunken parent had beaten them and thrust them out of the house. Some, rescued by the Society for the Prevention of Cruelty to Children, were literally lifted from the den of misery they called a home, at times after an actual fight with parents who did not wish to lose a child who supported them by begging or by theft.

Once a policeman came to Father Drumgoole with a note from a magistrate: would he take in two children who had been refused by several institutions because of their horrible condition? Father Drumgoole looked at the pair held by the officer in a tight grip. They were indeed filthy, their hair, long and matted and evidently not combed for weeks, all but covering their distrustful, fearful eyes. He judged they were about six and eight years old.

Father Drumgoole noted how close together they stood and how evidently they were attached to each other, as the officer explained, "I've been after them all day. They live under the market and they managed to hide from everybody in the daytime. Been doing it for weeks."

"Under the market?" Father Drumgoole was incredulous.

The officer nodded. "They came out nights and lived mostly, I guess, on skins of fruit and bad vegetables. This morning we set a trap to catch them. We stopped up the openings under the market till we found the two in one hole. So here they are. You'll take them?"

Father Drumgoole agreed, and the officer made ready to leave. This time they clung to him. "We want to go home!" said the older. "My brother and me want to go now."

Father Drumgoole's heart ached for the little boys. Their home was only a hole in the ground but they had felt safe there—and together. Finally he persuaded them to let his helpers take them to the lavatory, cut their hair, wash and dress them in clean clothes. It was almost suppertime, and as each was made ready, he was sent to the playroom to join the other small children. Suddenly from the room came the sound of weeping. It was the newcomers both crying, "Where's my brother? I want my brother."

They had passed each other several times, but were so changed they had not recognized one another. Father Drumgoole, who had been keeping an eye on them, came into the room and one child ran up to him. "Where's my brother? You took him away. Bring him back. He needs me," he cried.

Father Drumgoole called the younger child and asked his name. "Now say it very loudly so this other boy can hear you." Then, for the first time, each recognized the other and they ran to the shelter of each other's arms. And that night they slept together in one cot. As Father Drumgoole, after his customary rounds of the dormitory, went back to his own room he was thinking of something he had read that day—a sentence by Horace Mann: "If an institution saved only one boy it would be worth all the cost and labor of setting it up. And if anyone thinks that an extravagant statement I would tell them, 'Not if it was my boy—or yours!' "

Of course this was the echo of his own feelings. Other boys were rude and reckless, perhaps the cost of more pains than they would ever know, but to save "my boy" was worth all the toil and the wealth in the world. And then Father Drumgoole smiled at himself, for he knew that every single boy in his Home and all the homeless ones in the streets were to him "my boy."

Late that summer Lord Rosebery came again to visit the Home. By this time he was becoming an important figure in English political life and was the close associate of Gladstone.

He told Father Drumgoole he had been traveling in Cuba and in the southern part of the States. But he thought he liked it better in the north of the country, for he was meeting such interesting people. There was Julia Ward Howe. "I love the sweep of her 'Battle Hymn.'" And Dr. Holmes and A. T. Stewart, and President Grant. "He told me he had that day shaken hands with eight thousand people," Lord Rosebery said of the latter. "Arithmetic stands aghast."

He had liked Longfellow very much and had gone to visit him for the second time. They had an amusing talk and the poet had proudly showed the Englishman his greatest treasure: a bit of Dante's coffin.

"I like it very much in your country," Rosebery summed up. "In Europe a man is made noble by his house and his retinue. Here he can be noble in spite of them."

He was shown the improvements in the Home since his last visit and told about the future plans for building. When he asked Father Drumgoole if he had got to Rome yet, the latter shook his head. "No, not yet," he said.

"I was back there last year," said Rosebery, "and I thought of you when I was in the Farnese Palace looking at the Christ in Raphael's Transfiguration."

Father Drumgoole knew the picture. "It is one of my favorites," he said. "The face is wonderful."

Lord Rosebery nodded. "Yes, it is. It is a face worn with the cares of ordinary life yet lit with an immortal compassion. Still you can see that the idea of mortality is there, too. You must see the original someday, Father. Any chance of that soon?"

Father Drumgoole shrugged his shoulders and waved toward the boys gathering for supper. "You see where my duty lies. Even to get away for a day is difficult."

Christmas Day of 1876 found Father Drumgoole, for the first time in his life, feeling very tired. He told himself that the reason was very simple: it was just that he had had a rather hard day. On Christmas Eve he had spent hours in the confessional and then had gone to the chapel to say his night prayers. After visiting the dormitory, he had retired around eleven o'clock.

At three-thirty he had to be up again, and he found it very difficult to rise. When he entered the chapel it was brightly lit by many candles and every gas jet was ablaze. Four hundred boys were there, some of them still very sleepy. They had been taught to be very quiet in the chapel and usually they were, but his appearance this morning was too much for them. From all sides he heard voices calling to him, "Merry Christmas, Father John. Merry Christmas, Father."

He stopped his preparations for Mass to smile at them and to return their greetings, for he had himself forgotten in the joy of the day the rule of the Home. In fact, before he began Mass he went down the chapel aisle and greeted the children in each pew. The smallest ones reached out to catch his sleeve, and some held on until he patted them on the cheek and gave them a smile.

After the first Mass he preached a short sermon, telling them what the day meant and that they should all love the Christ Child whose birthday it was. The children remained for his three Masses and were wonderfully good and quiet.

At seven there was a fine breakfast and then a distribution of clothing. By nine o'clock the smaller boys were all newly outfitted. One asked in surprise, "Did all this come down the chimney?" as he looked with disbelief at the big sooty fireplace and his own clean new suit.

On the morning after Christmas Father Drumgoole did not feel at all well. Nor was he better during the weeks that followed. By February those about him told him they thought he looked really ill. He scoffed at the idea but finally he allowed them to send for Dr. Welch from St. Vincent's Hospital, and the doctor, after examining him, said decidedly, "You must come right up to the hospital so that you can have proper care. You have no real illness but you seem all worn out."

Father Drumgoole was aghast at this suggestion, for it was clear he did not consider it in order. "I can't do that—not possibly. I haven't the time. And I'll get good care here. Just tell me what to do and I'll do it—but right here."

Dr. Welch looked skeptical but it was clear that nothing would persuade Father Drumgoole to leave the house. His physician felt reasonably certain that the "good care" would be little or none at all.

There was a very simple reason for Father Drumgoole's condition. He was overworked. In addition to his usual duties at the Home he had been trying to answer personally the thousands of letters that poured in regarding membership in St. Joseph's Union, and to thank people for their contributions, and this he had been doing for more than a year. Even though form letters and a circular had been printed for this purpose, he still felt he must add a few words before the letters were mailed. "I am very thankful to you for your kindness," ran one such handwritten message, "in aiding our work of charity as well as for the interest you take in it. Our new Home will soon, we hope, be going up. I place you and the members of your family in the Sacred Heart of Jesus." This, in varying forms, was the gist of his letters, and had there been but one or a few or even fifty it might not have been tiring, but they ran into many hundreds.

After a busy day at the Home he would sit up half the night writing. Then he would rise for an early Mass. He had given the members of the Union a promise: he would say Masses for them as long as he could stand. This was one reason he had refused to go to the hospital: he knew they might keep him in bed and for some time.

Now that he was so visibly exhausted by his task, friends offered their help with the heavy correspondence. Mr. Dougherty and others who came for this purpose were appalled at what they found as they went deeper into the mass of mail. In the avalanche of letters not yet answered there was even found a considerable amount of money.

"Have you been opening all these letters by yourself?" Father Drumgoole was asked.

"Of course not. I have plenty of helpers," said Father Drumgoole. But his friends were not reassured when they learned who these helpers were—strays who had come to the Home for a meal or with a hard-luck story. How much money had been lost to some of these "helpers" there was no way of knowing.

The group of businessmen now came to the Home evenings, opened the letters, noted down the amounts received, and kept the records and files. Father Drumgoole was delighted with the efficient way in which his burden had been eased, and realizing that these men were coming at a considerable sacrifice of time, he suggested that their methods be adopted and that William Cahill, once his altar boy and for some years a schoolteacher, be employed to take over the work and give the businessmen a rest. Mr. Dougherty approved the choice, noting in his daybook that "Billy is an enemy to no one but himself and thoroughly honest."

A little later two more men were employed, both at the suggestion of Mr. Dougherty. Though pleased that his advice was taken, Mr. Dougherty thought sadly that his innocent friend would have agreed just as easily to anyone mentioned to him and without ever asking about honesty or training.

Now Billy Cahill and his two cohorts answered all letters except those which clearly called for a reply from Father Drumgoole. And Billy also kept a watchful eye on the "helpers" brought in from time to time by Father Drumgoole.

On the second day of Billy's employment at the Home another complication had been discovered. When he reached the Home in the morning he found a great pile of letters lying on the floor of the entrance hall. Evidently the wooden box on the wall had proved much too small for the flood of mail and the postman simply dropped the overflow on the floor. Billy gathered the envelopes up and found in the one morning's mail more than $1,000. That afternoon a large mailbox with a good strong lock was rented from the post office and after that Box 3502 became known as "the Mission Box."

In such simple ways did the business methods of the Union develop. Best of all was the fact that help in answering his mountainous correspondence gave Father Drumgoole a chance to get some rest. By early summer he was his old strong self again.

Perhaps such incidents inclined him to feel that he ought to have a group of trustees for his work, so that he could consult with them when the occasion arose and get their advice. He therefore invited some of those who worked with him, including two of his cousins, Bernard and William Reilly, to join such a group.

In May 1877, under the laws of New York State, the group was made into a corporate society, to be named the Mission of the Immaculate Virgin for the Protection of Homeless and Destitute Children. Seven trustees were named for the first year—Matthew Leavy, the two Reillys, James O'Neill, Hugh O'Donnell, James Dougherty, and Father Drumgoole.

However, as time went on the trustees found very little to do in the way of "managing the concerns of the Society," as their duties were defined. It really remained the one-man concern it had been from the beginning. The members were sometimes to complain of this in later years but only to each other. Sometimes the unbusinesslike methods of Father Drumgoole irritated these businessmen, but the simple fact was that his methods were successful, no matter how unorthodox.

At last, in July 1877, appeared Volume I, Number 1, of *The Homeless Child and Messenger of St. Joseph's Union*. It had been delayed beyond the promised time of publication, the chief reason being that Father Drumgoole wrote or edited its entire contents and had been so busy that it was only now that he had been able to assemble the material for this first number.

It was a well-printed, sixteen-page publication, in format more like a newspaper than a magazine. The cover of the first issue carried a picture of Archbishop McCloskey and the second page an account of his installation in September 1875 as the first cardinal in the United States, and the speech which he gave at his titular church in Rome—Santa Maria sopra Minerva.

Then followed the report Father Drumgoole had made to the Cardinal at the beginning of the year and in which he gave a concrete account of the work carried out at the Home during the six years of its existence. During that time more than 5,000 boys had been sheltered there; a thousand of them had been prepared for the Sacraments; many of the children made their Communions often during the year, and even those who were in the Home for only a brief time had the opportunity, through attending Mass and through his brief instructions, to acquire some knowledge of the Faith.

Despite the addition of 55 Warren Street, he reported, the Home was much too small. The location was not very good either, for many of the boys had to come a long way from their work. This difficulty, however, would be ended when the new Home was erected.

His night school was paying dividends, too. Boys who had not even known the alphabet when they came were now able to read and cipher, and this would mean they could secure better jobs. He reminded the Cardinal that when a boy's salary reached six dollars a week, the rule was that he must leave the Home and seek a boarding-house. But he gave assurance that the new home was first investigated to make sure that the boy would be in good hands.

Of the small children who were staying in the Home,

since they had had no other nor was there room elsewhere, some would make their First Communions soon. "They are truly the children of Jesus Christ," he wrote, "having no friends outside the Home. I believe they have brought the blessing of God into the Home with them." Some had been adopted; the rest would remain with him.

He did not add that, as soon as it was known that he had received some destitute children, others were brought to him when admittance was refused elsewhere, and that the courts sometimes asked him to take a child. With these he received much help from the Conferences and the Catholic Union, the lay women who were his constant aids, and from the religious, too, despite the fact that they already had their hands full.

He listed for the Cardinal more than 50,000 free meals given that year and more than 16,000 free lodgings. Many of the poor applied for food every day and were given food. "No person has to my knowledge been refused relief in our institution," he wrote, with the one evidence of pride manifested in his report.

The city was supposed to help with the children's care with money raised through the excise tax, but less than a third to which the Home was entitled had been sent him. And of course there were many expenses outside the running of the house. Father Drumgoole listed the large printers' bills, the circulars and pamphlets dealing with the Union, and the cost of stationery and mailing, for he tried to communicate each year with every one of the thousands of members of the Union.

"But the Union is in a flourishing condition," the report ended, "and I hope to be able to purchase our building lots by the beginning of the year. I have a good balance with which to begin."

The first issue of *The Homeless Child* carried an account of the famous bazaar, and an article on the Mass by a member of the Union. It also reprinted the statement of Mr. Letchworth, Commissioner of Charities in New York, written after his interview with Father Drumgoole, and his very laudatory report on the conditions he had found during his visitation of the Home.

The final pages were devoted to the work of the Union, with a conscientious statement of the finances—receipts and expenses—of the Home. For Father Drumgoole felt that each member had the right to know the facts since through his yearly contribution he had become a stockholder in the Home.

In 1876 Father Drumgoole had been asked to speak at a meeting of the Social Service Association at Saratoga Springs. His brief talk had made such a fine impression and his remarks expressed such an understanding of the problem of the vagrant child that he was asked to return in October of the following year and give a long address. Most of those at the meeting were not of his religion but not many differed from him in the opinions he expressed.

"The heart is the battlefield of the soul," he said. "It is there that the struggle between vice and virtue takes place. It is there that the foundation of a good or bad life is laid. We may spend millions of dollars to better the condition of the child and if the heart is not cultivated, all is lost. The vices of youth will predominate in manhood and he may easily fall a prey to the prevailing spirit of insubordination and to all the terrible isms of the day which are everywhere threatening the peace of society. If you want good and valiant soldiers, cultivate the heart. If you want honest voters, politicians, and legislators, who will faithfully perform their duties and be governed in their actions more by the justice of God and the welfare of the country than by sordid and corrupt motives, then I say again, cultivate the heart of the child. All that children want are kind acts and kind words to make them an honor to the country."

Those present recognized that his words were backed by long experience, for they knew or had been told of his work. His were not the vague speculations of the theorist but the result of long and close intimacy with boys of the streets, with the forgotten, neglected waifs of a great city.

He referred, too, to the opinion of many people that there was a better method of reclamation than by institutions, that these had failed, and that families—especially families in the West and Midwest—could better train these children. In one year 4,000 New York City children had been placed in Western homes, he said, no doubt many in good homes, but there was little proof of the results.

"What advantage do they have which the East does not have?" Father Drumgoole asked of his audience. "Do they have superior facilities for child care or a finer and higher morality? Are they more virtuous and larger-hearted out there? Surely our schools and churches and homes of refuge are not inferior to those in the West. Why must a child be packed off to the West to be properly brought up?

"This I do know," he added earnestly. "Many children are sent there and are never heard from again, and the Children's Aid Society knows it. Inquiries about them have proved fruitless."

A general discussion followed about the New York law of 1875, which provided that if a child were placed in any institution or home it should be, whenever possible, in one of the same faith as that of the parents of the child.

When Father Drumgoole was asked his opinion on this matter, he said, "I think the legislature acted wisely when it left destitute young children to be brought up by those of their own persuasion whenever it could be done. I think last year's amendment making this law optional with the magistrate was very unfortunate. It would always be a consolation to the soldier who rushes to his country's call to know that should he fail to return his family will grow up bearing their father's name among their own kindred and in the same faith as his, whether he was Methodist, Episcopalian, or Catholic."

On the way back to New York he was still thinking of this matter of the dependent child, subject to a law that could be changed at the will of the party or faith which happened to be more powerful. How the rights of the child were ignored, he thought sadly, by legislation like this which in one year gave to such a child its basic religious rights and the next year all but took them away by making the child's religious future "optional" with the magistrate who was committing the child.

There was one thing he could do about this unfair legislation, he decided: he could speak to city voters. During the next weeks he asked many of the Vincentians to speak about this matter in sodalities and clubrooms and before labor groups. He himself gave brief talks on the subject, sometimes several in a single evening, urging the voters to send to the legislature men who would not allow any interference with the basic law of the free exercise and enjoyment of religion.

"This law," he said one evening, "allowing people to pack off poor children from their homes and put them where they can be fed and housed at least cost to the state, and with no regard for their faith—is it fair? Is it sensible? What is this but punishing poverty in the child as if it were a serious sin?"

Life went on at the Home with no major crises. Help was always coming from unexpected sources, as people read about the Home or came to see this unusual institution. Among Father Drumgoole's faithful helpers were groups of women from the neighborhood who met at one another's houses to repair the clothing which they collected for the boys. They made the bread for the Warren Street house. And all over New York the promoters for the Union were collecting money.

The months were punctuated with parties on feast days and holidays—Our Lady's feasts, those of St. Joseph, Independence Day. There was the big Thanksgiving dinner with its weary servers gathering afterward for a cup of coffee in the room of the apparently unwearied Father Drumgoole who had worked harder than any of them.

There was especially the Christmas celebration, and of the one in the year 1877 Father Drumgoole was very proud, for on that day nearly a hundred children made their First Communions. The beautifully decked chapel was filled mostly with working boys but there were many small ones among them now, some so little they had to be lifted into the pews.

The first Mass that morning was sung by a chorus made up entirely of children in the Home. A seven-year-old, with a clear lovely soprano, sang the "Adeste Fidelis," and, as Father Drumgoole listened to the childish voice calling the faithful to come to Bethlehem, he knew how those words really meant *all* the faithful, and that included his children, children who had come to him in filthy rags and were now cleanly clad and warm. His prayer that morning was an insistent one. On a huge tree in the library he had gifts for the children, but he wanted a gift for himself, too, on this day: money for the new Home, so that many more little children could come to this Bethlehem.

Father Drumgoole was always happy when he sat among his children or knelt before the altar with them or saw them warm in their beds. But of course he could never be entirely happy when in his mind's eye he saw those outside this circle of warmth, the ones who had no shelter at all from the bitter winds and cheerless streets of winter or the burning pavements of summer.

10

>>

The Home Overflows—Plans for
a New One

ON DECEMBER 31, 1878, Father Drumgoole announced that
St. Joseph's Union had acquired four city lots for the new
building. It had taken a little longer than he had expected
to find the location and to make this purchase, but it had
been something worth waiting for, for the property he had
in the end obtained was excellent. The lots were situated
at the corners of Great Jones and Lafayette streets, about
a mile from the Warren Street Home; they had belonged
to the Episcopal parish of St. Bartholomew, and the old
church on the site was still standing though in so bad a
state of repair that it would have to be pulled down.

The cost of the lots was $68,987.20, he wrote to the
members of the Union. He told them it was their property,
for each of them had helped in its purchase, and he was
offering it in their name as a gift to St. Joseph for Our
Lady. He added that, true to his earlier promise to them,
the property was paid for in full, cash down. What he did
not tell was that at that moment what was left in the coffers
of the Union was exactly fifty-seven dollars!

Late in the afternoon of the day of purchase a group
gathered about the old church on the newly bought lots
for a little ceremony in honor of the event. The old bell
which still hung in the steeple rang a merry peal to cele-

brate the acquisition of the land to which more than three hundred thousand members of the Union had contributed —in the United States, the West Indies, Australia, South America, and all over Europe.

On January 23, 1879, the feast of the Espousals of Mary and Joseph, a High Mass of thanksgiving was celebrated at the Home. The children's choir sang the hymn which Father Drumgoole loved best of all—"Hail Virgin, dearest Mary." When the Mass was over, Father Drumgoole knelt before Our Lady's statue, aglow with many lights and surrounded with flowers, and presented the deed of the property to her, for the Home was indeed to be hers. The new building would have the title of Mission of the Immaculate Virgin.

He sang the first lines of the dedication:

> "Oh, Mary, my beautiful Mother,
> This day we give thee our gift,"

and, as he laid the parchment at her feet, the children's voices took up the hymn and sang it to the end. The deed was to lie in that place for an entire year, and Father Drumgoole hoped fervently that at that time another gift could be brought to her—a new home for the new site.

That summer proved unusually hot, but the boys at the Home cooled off in the evenings on the roof where, under a big awning, they enjoyed the breezes from the river. And that summer began the trips on the Hudson which were to become such happy events for countless children.

One hot August day Father Drumgoole chartered the steamer *Blackbird* and took the children up the river, inviting a few grownups to come along to help him. A trio composed of harp, violin, and flute played, and the chil-

dren sang most of the way, a happy mingling of Irish airs
and hymns. At Alderney Park they all disembarked and
lunch was served in the picnic grove—ham and tongue and
bread and butter and lemonade for the children, and
bottles of Belfast Ale for the older people. Then the party
went home, tired and hot and happy.

"Music only nine dollars and certainly worth it," commented Mr. Dougherty in his diary that evening, "and a
better-behaved lot of children I never saw."

All that summer Father Drumgoole took walks down to
his vacant lots, where the old church was in process of
demolition. No new building was to be immediately
erected, but the plans were ready.

"The more miserable the homeless and destitute are
when you meet them the more they resemble Him," he
wrote at that time in a leaflet sent to the members of the
Union and to others he hoped would become members.
"Happy are those who will help to erect a home to shelter
Christ in the person of the poor and homeless and destitute
Christ."

During those days his mind was filled with plans for the
new building. Bids were being received, with great differ-
ences in the estimates presented. This was a part of the
work he hated to deal with, for the "building business"
bored him. What he wanted was to find someone in whom
he could have confidence; all about him were people urging on him their favorite contractors.

One day he asked Mr. Dougherty to take a day off from
his lumber business and go to Staten Island with him.

"I've heard it's a pleasant place and I can get away from
bids and bidders and friends of bidders for a few hours
there," he said. Mr. Dougherty had been about ready to

produce the name of his own pet builder but prudently decided that this was not the right time.

"Get a contented mind," he advised Father Drumgoole, as they sat on the upper deck of the ferry, the wind on their faces. "And if you have that it won't matter if Tom the Devil does the work."

The trip on the water helped calm Father Drumgoole, and the brief time they spent on the island, riding about in a little rig, was pleasant, too. The one thing he regretted on the way home was that the boys had not been along to enjoy it. "Someday we'll have a trip and bring them along," he comforted himself as he watched the island disappearing and New York coming nearer.

Early in September 200 of the older boys, together with many members of St. Joseph's Union who lived in New York, made the Jubilee visits at the appointed churches. They made a really imposing procession, and many watched them as they marched along. When Father Drumgoole saw the people lining the streets his heart was happy, for in their faces was not only interest but approval at the sight of these nicely dressed children, these healthy, well-mannered boys. He felt all the pride of a father in his own sons as he watched the lines swinging along, carrying at their head a banner on which was inscribed, "Come, all ye faithful, make the Jubilee. It will do more for your souls than all the wealth of this land can do for your bodies."

As they marched up Broadway, across Grand Street, and down Mulberry, they sang hymns. When they came to Lafayette Street, the whole line stopped as if at an unspoken order, and all stood for a few moments looking in silence at their future home.

That evening Father Drumgoole listed for the diocesan record some of the year's educational work: fourteen divisions of catechism classes, several singing classes, daily school at St. Peter's for the boys too young to go to work, evening classes for the rest.

He also stated that a half million copies of *The Homeless Child* had been printed that year. He thought the last issue had been very fine; one man who had seen its handsome format said to him, "For a homeless child it is very finely dressed."

Those who heard of this incredible circulation often wondered just how the work entailed was ever accomplished. The quarters in the old building were getting very crowded; it seemed impossible that the work of mailing, of answering letters, of recording new members, could be done at all in the space at their disposal. There were some who rather leaned to the assumption that St. Joseph and Father Drumgoole worked on it together during the night.

The membership of the Union was also incredible. There were many members in the metropolis; New York's fancy had been caught, for many remembered the unforgettable bazaar of 1875 and its myriad prizes. But the membership of the Union went far beyond New York. The members were legion now and they were everywhere in the world. Pope Pius IX had been a member and now Leo XIII was one. Daniel O'Connell belonged to the Union. Members of the hierarchy all over the world had joined. Priests and journalists, generals and admirals, nuns and brothers were enrolled, as well as many thousands more.

From Molokai, Father Damien had sent a contribution which automatically made him a member. In Italy, Don Bosco enrolled and wrote, "Don't forget us, but let a continual exchange of prayer pass between old Europe and young America."

And it was from all these thousands, from the small sums contributed yearly, that would come the great new Home soon to be built. From these small sums came the meals and shelter for the children as well as for Father Drumgoole's newest project of all—a home for the smallest ones and for the occasional girls who were sent to him. From these sums were paid the workers at the Home and from them the poor were fed. Everything came from the contributions of twenty-five cents a year to the Union.

The latest project—the shelter for the smallest children and the girls—was in charge of the very efficient Miss McGinn and of several helpers. This was located at Fort Washington, far up the Hudson. The estate on which the children were kept did not belong to Father Drumgoole, but was a property which, due to a legal dispute over a mortgage, they were allowed to occupy rent free until the matter was cleared up. To Miss McGinn Father Drumgoole entrusted his little city children. The place was a godsend to them—the big shabby house that sheltered them, the wide grounds where they could tumble on the grass, the fine river breezes that put color into their pale cheeks.

One day when Father Drumgoole came to look over the place, and more particularly to bring toys and candy to the children, Miss McGinn told him an amusing story she had just learned about the previous owner, a titled gentleman, who had lived there alone and completely ignored the relatives who were hopefully waiting to share his estate when he passed away.

He had inserted his own death notice in the paper and at the same time made a will which entirely disinherited

them all. At his supposed funeral he armed his two valets
and had them mount guard over an empty coffin. No one
was allowed to look at the corpse until the will had been
read. The relatives who had come mainly to learn how the
estate would be divided listened to the lawyer reading it,
and the grief on their faces changed to indignation when
they heard that some were cut off with very little and some
with nothing.

While they were still giving voice to their disappointment and anger, the "corpse" descended the stairs from
the attic, confronted his dumfounded relatives and told
them exactly what he thought of them. They hastily departed in their coaches, as poor as when they came, and
the Count disposed of his coffin and lived happily for the
rest of his days. And now there was considerable litigation
over his estate, and the orphans profited by living there
free.

One fact which was not much publicized was the re-
markable number of conversions brought about by the
work at the Home. To know that the Church is on the
side of the poor and hungry, to know that it fed and
sheltered them, was a powerful argument, stronger than
theological discussion. Then, too, it made those Catholics
who saw what had been accomplished with these children
of the streets more energetic in helping the waifs in their
own neighborhood, for many of them had not been aware
of conditions until they were confronted with the remedy.

By the autumn of 1879 workmen had pulled down the
last of the old church on the new property. It had been
planned that the cornerstone of the new Home would be
laid on December 14, and a large platform had been
erected for the notables who would attend. But on that

day the weather was so bad that the ceremony could not be held. Many were greatly disappointed at its curtailment and none more than Father Drumgoole, who had planned to have Gilmore's Band play its finest tunes. He had engaged it long before, and Mr. Gilmore—"like the gentleman he is," said the grateful Father Drumgoole—refused to charge him anything.

The next day the weather cleared and the affair could be held. The site was blessed by Monsignor Quinn, representing the Cardinal, and a box, previously blessed by Cardinal McCloskey, was placed inside the cornerstone. Within this box, covered with red silk and embroidered with two hearts, were pictures of Pope Leo XIII, the New York Cardinal, and other American prelates, as well as coins and medals minted that year, and a file of Catholic and general newspapers, including *The Homeless Child*. There were also a guide to New York with maps and a copy of the national anthem with Gilmore's musical score.

A carriage had been sent for Monsignor Quinn and a new ritual bought for his use at the ceremony. When Father Drumgoole handed it to him, after hurriedly picking out the page containing the blessing for the occasion, Monsignor Quinn began to read. Suddenly he stopped. "Why, Father John, you have me blessing a railroad," he said, and hunted about until he found the proper prayer.

Father Drumgoole's prayer that Christmas was for more funds so that his building might soon rise over his fine but at present useless lots. The prayer did not stop with the feast alone, but went right on into the new year. During the day, whenever he found time, he talked to one or the other of his Patrons; at night he prayed for more room for his large family, growing larger each day. "Go to St.

Joseph," his constant advice to others, he also took himself. But he went so often that sometimes he thought sadly
St. Joseph must weary of his importunities.

"I suppose he says sometimes, 'If I don't give this fellow
what he wants he'll bother the life out of me,' and so I get
it," he said to Mr. Dougherty one day. And when a visiting
Bishop remarked, "You must have a gold mine around
here somewhere," Father Drumgoole said solemnly, "Yes,
I have one—but St. Joseph has the key."

Except for his long talks with his Patron, his times of
prayer in the chapel, his breviary, his life was as simple as
were his meals, and those were far too simple to please
those who worked with him. His breakfast was oatmeal
and coffee. Dinner was whatever plain food they gave him,
and then he ate nothing more until breakfast the next
day. His bed was the one he had found when first he came
to the house; it had no springs, only slats and a mattress
filled with straw. Several times when his friends tried to
replace the old furniture in his room he vetoed their
efforts. He was very comfortable, he said. But if they
wished to give the price of such proposed gifts to the
Home, that was a different matter, and he would accept
gladly.

11

The Mission of the Immaculate Virgin

THE LAND on Lafayette Street had been bought, the church pulled down. It was when the subject of building came up that Father Drumgoole met with trouble. For what he envisioned was not the ordinary three- or four-story building of the day. The new Home was to have eight stories as well as a basement and an attic. And each room must have at least two windows.

"You are trying to build the first skyscraper in lower New York," his contractor had said when he studied the plans, and there was misgiving in his voice. It was true that Father Drumgoole himself had looked with some awe at the plans when he saw them worked out—each detail, of course, revolving about the comfort and well being of the children who were to live there.

To the surprise of many he was planning that each child should have his own cubicle surrounded by a five-foot partition for privacy. Each cubicle was to contain a bed, a chair, a washstand with basin and pitcher, and each child was to have his own locker and key. He met all arguments with his own and eventually he had his way in everything he wanted, despite architects and contractors.

The building of the new Home was begun late in 1879, and continued except when the weather brought it to a

halt. By January of the next year the basement was completed and one wing built to the second story. Father
Drumgoole's dream was to have it finished by August so
that the children could be moved before the winter came.

Many people stopped to watch the progress of the building and asked questions about its purpose as they studied
its amazing height. Father Drumgoole who was often at
hand, was happy to answer all such inquiries for just as
a guide knows his castles and museums, he was familiar
with its every dimension and the use of each part.

The dimensions were 128 feet long and 78 feet wide,
and the height 128 feet, he would inform visitors. Its basement would have kitchens, dining room, bathrooms; the
first floor, chapel, director's room, guest room, publications room. The second floor would house the study and
classrooms, the reading room, the library. The rest of the
floors would be devoted to the children living in the
Home. It would be steam-heated and the materials for the
construction were brick and cement.

Father Drumgoole especially liked to show to members
of St. Joseph's Union the drawings of the rooms which
were to house the business of the Union, now grown to
colossal proportions. Two million pieces of mail had been
sent out during the past year, and the workers in their
small space on Warren Street were eagerly awaiting the
day when they could occupy their new quarters.

But he found time for many other things that summer
of 1880. The excursions took place as usual. And once
when a party was given for the children of the City Idiot
Asylum and the hospital children on Randalls Island the
choir from Father Drumgoole's Home was invited and
sang gay songs while young members of the Union distributed ice cream and cake. The hospital children gave

generous applause and demanded encores from their delighted entertainers.

It was a very fine party, but perhaps what especially pleased Father Drumgoole was to note that these Asylum children too were receiving fine care, that they were so evidently happy. For the city was growing more aware of its duty to its dependent children.

"A place like this is a credit to New York," he said to Father Gelinas, the hospital chaplain. "The poorest and most neglected child will respond to kindness and love. When every institution realizes that——" And he sighed even as he spoke, knowing that this place was an exception and knowing, too, that there were still many utterly friendless children on the streets, children cast on the waves with no spar to cling to unless someone came in time to save them.

The summer excursion on September 8 was a fine sight. Four divisions of boys, each in charge of a prefect, marched in formation, dressed in black trousers, white coats, and new straw hats, at their head two banners, one with a painting of Our Lady, the other of St. Joseph and the Child. Down Broadway and Cortlandt Street people watched with interest as the orderly procession passed, clean, nicely dressed, looking not at all like waifs of the city streets, but like boarders from a private school. Boys and invited guests, there were in all more than 400 in the long line.

At Starr's Wharf a big barge was waiting with the tug *Chamberlain*. It was a warm day but the air was bracing as they set off to the playing of flute and violin, harp, and Irish pipes. The boat picked up Miss McGinn and the children at Fort Washington and then sailed up the Hudson, everyone singing as loudly as they could. Passing barges cheered the gay party and waved handkerchiefs in greeting.

Father Drumgoole was everywhere, smiling to see the happiness about him. There was only one wish in his heart: that every member of the Union all the world over might see their boys that day.

In 1880 Thanksgiving was celebrated for the last time in the old Home, and a big party was planned. All the former boys were invited to dinner and almost 400 came to eat the 500 pounds of turkey and 200 pounds of beef and ham that had been provided. The Union, too, was well represented, at least one member from every state in the country having come for the occasion.

Father Drumgoole had a very good report to make them. During that year there had not been one death at the Home; in fact, there had been no serious illness. And during that year he had had the joy of seeing eighty children restored to their parents or adopted by friends.

After dinner the boys, who knew how he loved singing, had arranged in his honor a fine medley of all his favorite melodies: "Hymn to America," "Mother Dear," "Hail Columbia" and, last of all, "Hail, Holy Joseph, Hail." Afterward he gave them a little talk about the true meaning of patriotism, how this was, in a way, the expression of thankfulness for the gifts America gave its citizens.

"When you grow old enough to vote," he said, "you must remember, you must realize, that you are called on to defend by your votes the liberty for which your fathers fought and died and thus uphold the honor and glory of your country. This is patriotism."

That day he had received a letter from Archbishop Gibbons in Baltimore. He wanted to read it aloud to the assembled boys but felt it was too laudatory to himself. It expressed the deep—almost the anxious—hope that God would spare Father Drumgoole to finish his building. "You will be the instrument of God to save many souls," the letter ended.

One day, when the new Home was almost ready, the *Times* sent a reporter to get a story about it. When he asked Father Drumgoole just how he had happened to undertake such a project, he received a very matter-of-fact answer. "Oh, I always meant to do something like this from the time I came to the Newsboys' Home. But I had no money and at first did not know how to go about getting it. Then I decided to hold a big bazaar and made ten thousand dollars and with several additional gifts I got started. I was still a long way from my goal, so I organized a society and started a little magazine that sold at twenty-five cents a year. That is how I got the money for this building. You can say it was built with quarter dollars."

The reporter listened with respect to this simple success story and looked almost with disbelief at the tall building rising a few blocks away. He hoped devoutly that in the new building access to Father Drumgoole's office would be easier, for now one had to go up two flights of steps—steep ones, too—through a big room, then a small and terribly crowded office—that of the Union—and into the extremely little room that was Father Drumgoole's office and bedroom and dining room and where he received all callers. There was still the iron bedstead, the little table with the green cloth piled with papers and letters, and to one side a white napkin spread out under a thick blue china cup and saucer and a pepper and salt shaker.

It was very ordinary and plain, and the priest looked ordinary and plain, too, in his worn suit, with his carelessly cut hair. But one forgot the room and the plainness when one looked into the smiling face with its tonsure-like fringe of light hair, the wonderfully kind but searching eyes, the mobile mouth. The reporter realized, suddenly, why the old Home had been such a success and why the new one would be, too.

While they were talking a whirring was heard in the room, and as the startled reporter looked around, he heard a tiny voice saying, "Cuckoo, cuckoo." Father Drumgoole chuckled at his surprise and went to an open door, pulled it closed, and there was the noisemaker—an old cuckoo clock.

It gave him much amusement when someone was startled at hearing this for the first time. His boys and his helpers were used to it but the unseen voice always surprised a stranger in the room. The clock was one of his few childhood mementoes, a gift to his mother, and had hung for years in the rooms on Mott Street.

He took the reporter to the new Home and showed him the new offices of the Union—fine big rooms with many desks and counters. Father Drumgoole himself gazed at them with awe. "It looks almost like a bank, doesn't it?" he said.

Some months earlier every paper in the city had printed a story about the new Home's water supply. So now the reporter asked, "Is your water supply still holding up?"

"Oh, yes," smiled Father Drumgoole, "we have enough and more than we need."

The story of the artesian well at the new Home was known all over New York, for it was the first that had been sunk in that part of the city. The previous winter Father Drumgoole had begun the task of providing for a good water supply. When he decided upon the sinking of an artesian well, there was a shaking of heads. This had been tried more than once and had always proved a failure. But Father Drumgoole paid no attention to the prophets. He had consulted St. Joseph and apparently received approval, for the work went on. Finally, at 637 feet, the men struck water, a fine well, and evidently one which would not soon be exhausted.

The surprised objectors came to see. "Who did the work?" they asked. Father Drumgoole named the company.

No, no. They did not mean that. More than one had had the services of this company and without results. They wanted to know who had directed the work.

He smiled and said in an offhand way, "Oh, that. A very great man did that for me."

"Well, who is this very great man?" asked a hotel owner. "Will he sink a well for me? I'll pay him any amount, for I've had plenty of trouble with my water supply."

"Well, that I don't know—whether he'll do it."

"Tell me his name anyway."

"His name is St. Joseph. Ever heard of him?"

The puzzled hotel man shook his head. "But tell me how to get hold of him."

Father Drumgoole was suddenly serious. "By prayer," he said.

The hotel man understood at last. He gave Father Drumgoole a quizzical glance. "And it took a lot of machinery, too?"

But Father Drumgoole looked at him innocently. "No, very little really. We got the water quickly."

After hearing of the results obtained at the new Home, others tried sinking artesian wells in that part of the city, but it was evident they did not know how to enlist the help of St. Joseph. They found no water and Father Drumgoole's well long remained the pride and the puzzlement of New York City.

To complete the building took longer than had been planned, but early in December of 1881 the move could be made to Lafayette Street. The boys were taken there in small groups, and comfortably installed although the place was not quite ready.

Now the children were housed in two entirely separated groups. On one floor were the little ones who did not go to work, on other floors the boys who worked by day and studied by night. Even before the move, in the late fall, Father Drumgoole had opened evening classes in the new Home for his older boys and for other young men who did not live at the Home, his plan being to offer a good commercial education. He employed competent men as teachers, and was already preparing to open an employment agency for these students. He had found that often one boy found a job for another, for the older ones came back to the Home to tell of an opportunity for those still living there.

Father Drumgoole decided to continue sending the younger boys to the nearby parochial school, for he did not think it a good idea for them to attend classes and to live in the same building. It was better for them to mingle daily with the outside world and other children.

On Christmas Day the new chapel, which was to be named in honor of Our Lord, was not quite ready and could not be decorated for the occasion, but Father Drumgoole said his three Masses there. Already, on December 8, the first Mass had been offered in the chapel—a Mass of thanksgiving in every sense of the word, for there was no debt on the house, as there had been none on the lots.

Everything was entirely paid for, as Father Drumgoole had promised.

It had taken a sum close to $300,000 to build the new Mission. It was bought, built, and furnished without the need of asking the aid of wealthy men or for state subsidies. Only the twenty-five-cent subscriptions of the members of St. Joseph's Union had provided the funds for this accomplishment.

His gift to his boys that Christmas was the new Home. And he had himself received a fine present from the Cardinal: the appointment of a priest to assist him in his work. The newly ordained Father O'Sullivan arrived in time to say a fourth Mass on Christmas Day.

In the afternoon the boys sang carols and there were several speeches. Father Drumgoole read them a poem from the Boston *Pilot* on his favorite subject, St. Joseph, and then added a few words of his own. "The great St. Teresa said, 'St. Joseph always helps me beyond my prayers and hopes.' It seems that God grants to other saints the power of assisting us at special moments. But regarding St. Joseph, I know from experience that he can help us in all our needs. It is as though Our Lord would wish us to understand that, as He submitted to him on earth, so He is still pleased in heaven to grant his requests."

In April 1882 Cardinal McCloskey paid his first visit to the new Mission. First of all, he was taken to the sanctuary and seated on the throne prepared for him, and the boys of the Mission passed before him in a long line before they took their seats. Then one of the boys read an address of welcome in a clear, loud voice and the Cardinal, obviously moved, expressed his thanks and said this was a day of joy and happiness for him. Then the Cardinal was escorted about the building.

In the basement, he was fascinated by the great double range with its huge hundred-gallon tank.

"We use this to make soup for the poor," Father Drumgoole explained, and showed him the room set aside for them—"St. Joseph's Room"—where they came to eat.

The Cardinal drank some of the water from the famous artesian well. He greeted the engineer in the boiler room, and then was taken by elevator to the upper floors. On the second floor, where the cashier's office and mailing departments of the Union were installed, he opened his eyes wide in amazement at the volume of work being carried on there. He examined with delight the library on the second floor and promised to send some books for its shelves.

He was taken to the ninth floor—the playrooms—and to the laundry on the tenth, and last of all to the roof—a large playground enclosed with a strong iron railing. It was the first such roof playground ever built in the city.

The Cardinal looked out from the windows of the Mission over the roofs of Cooper Union and Mr. Stewart's department store, to the dome of the post office and the river. "You have the finest view in New York City," he said admiringly, and it was clear he was reluctant to leave. But he showed his weariness now, for it had been an extensive tour. He rested for a while in a room especially prepared for him, then, having blessed everything and everyone in the Mission, he departed.

The Cardinal promised to dedicate the new chapel the following month, on the feast of the Patronage of St. Joseph. To have him come again so soon was a matter for gratification, especially since he now suffered from serious heart trouble and was attending few functions. Father Drumgoole expressed by letter his grateful thanks: "By Your Eminence's presence you are treating these children as the royal children of Christ whom they so well represent. If they were children of princes of earth you could not have done more, and I feel that under the circumstances you could not have done as much."

On the morning of the dedication Father Drumgoole went into the chapel for one final look, to make sure all was ready for the distinguished guest. The altar was flower-decked; the Cardinal's throne draped in the papal white and gold. Opposite his throne was another for Archbishop Corrigan. The front pews were reserved for clergymen and the Sisters of Charity.

The procession included Monsignor Quinn and Monsignor Preston, and last of all the Archbishop in his cope. It circled the chapel and paused before the altar as Cardinal McCloskey, in pontifical robes, his crozier in his hand, appeared at the vestry door. He knelt on his *prie-dieu* while the Litany of the Saints was recited, then joined the procession as it made the round of the chapel.

The High Mass began, with Monsignor Farley acting as master of ceremonies. The papal benediction, received by cable a few hours before, was read: "Long life and prosperity and papal blessing to the Union and all those present this day."

Archbishop Corrigan's sermon was after Father Drumgoole's heart, for it dwelled chiefly on St. Joseph, recently proclaimed the Patron of the Universal Church. Then came the blessing of the house by the Archbishop, as the Cardinal had already overtaxed his strength by the long ceremony, having come, in fact, against the advice of his doctors.

He was living now at Mount St. Vincent, thirteen miles from the city, because of the state of his health. When some had tried to dissuade him from taking part in the ceremony of dedicating the chapel, he had told them, "If I can possibly stand on my feet I want to go through with this ceremony. It may be the last of my official life, and it is one I do not wish to miss. It would gratify me more to dedicate this chapel for homeless children than it did to dedicate the great new Cathedral."

In the afternoon a bronze statue of Our Lady was unveiled before the new building. A large platform had been built for the official guests and over the entrance of the Mission were to be seen the papal arms. The statue itself was draped in the American flag. Gilmore's Band played "Holy God We Praise Thy Name," followed by a medley of Irish airs.

Earlier someone had asked if Father Drumgoole would approve Irish airs played at a sacred ceremony of this kind, and when he was consulted, his blue eyes had sparkled. "Why not?" he asked. "*All* Irish music is sacred music."

The musical program was followed by a moment's deep silence. Then, after a trumpet blast, the drapery was pulled from the statue as from the upper windows of the Mission fell a shower of rose petals, scattered by the youngest children. The band played, "On this day, O beautiful Mother," its words taken up by the thousands of people who stood on the street watching the ceremony.

There was another silence, and then a cheer as Archbishop Corrigan, Father Drumgoole, and Dr. McGlynn appeared on the platform. The last named was to make the address and Father Drumgoole's voice was far from steady as he made his brief introduction. Father McGlynn was considered one of the best orators in New York by Catholics and Protestants alike, and he did not fail them on this occasion.

"This building," he said, "preaches the charity of Christ

as no words could do—except, perhaps, the words of Christ Himself, 'A new commandment I give unto you, that you love one another.' The work we gather to honor today exemplifies not only the general charity of Christ but the most touching quality of it—that which teaches us to throw around the helplessness of little children the panoply of His infinite goodness and power. 'As you have done it to the least of these, you have done it unto Me,' He said. And the care and attention and reverence we pay to the weakest and poorest He makes the basis of all we can hope for from Him in time and in eternity."

At the end he paid a tribute to Father Drumgoole: "He is like the theologians who went forth without scrip or staff to put down pagan Rome and raise up the downtrodden and oppressed. He belongs to the school of St. Vincent and St. Francis and I would almost be willing to make affidavit that he is twin to one of them. He is no doubt shocked at the eulogy I am compelled to pronounce but which I am sure every one of you will agree is not improperly spoken."

Applause drowned his next words—thundering applause of hand and voice, and the speaker waited, smiling, until it had died away. Then he ended, "Shall we not do our best to keep him? Shall we not pray God to preserve him so that he may live many a year and never make up His mind to let him die until He has found a man as good as himself to leave in his shoes."

Father Drumgoole, obviously overwhelmed at this totally unexpected tribute, read the papal blessing, and Archbishop Corrigan blessed the assembled people.

"And now Mr. Gilmore will do the rest," said Father Drumgoole. The bandmaster responded magnificently, first with opera selections and then with a special rendering of "Monastery Bells" which was greatly applauded. As a finale "Columbia" was played, the crowd taking up the words and singing lustily.

The statue met with universal approval. It was of bronze, eight feet in height, and the sculptor had depicted Our Lady exactly as Father Drumgoole had asked him to do. On her face was a look of welcoming love and her arms were extended as if she were inviting boys without number, or regard to age or condition, to enter the shelter and love of the Mission which bore her name.

❯❯

12

Mount Loretto

FATHER DRUMGOOLE's greatest dream had been fulfilled and he had his big Mission for children. Now he turned to other dreams, also dear to his heart.

One was the fostering of vocations. Since he had as yet found none among his boys, he decided to offer help and the hospitality of the Mission to two young aspirants to the priesthood who had been brought to his attention. These boys he entered at St. Xavier's College on West Fifteenth Street and they lived with him at the Mission, helping him as prefects during holidays and vacations. One, John G. McCormick, came from Newport and was working in the city when Father Drumgoole learned through a friend of the boy's ambition; the other, Charles Cassidy, had been placed by his widowed mother in a Catholic orphanage and was just fifteen when Father Drumgoole enrolled him at the college. He planned later to send them both to Our Lady of Angels' Seminary.

As soon as possible he hoped to open a special evening class where a young man with a vocation, but who had in the meantime to earn his living, could come to prepare for the seminary. For he had never forgotten his own struggle, the long years he had waited for his own ordination. If he could help young men, delayed in their studies for the priesthood by poverty or family obligations, this would be his way.

Another dream—that of a home in the country for his boys and girls—he never forgot either. He had merely pushed it aside. Now, with the city Mission realized, with the Union flourishing and in capable hands, with sufficient funds and the promise of their continuance, he began to give serious thought to a home in the country for the girls and the smaller children, those at Fort Washington and those still in the city Mission. It was all the more necessary because already, little more than a year after its completion, the wonderful skyscraper building was overcrowded, as packed as the old Home had been. Many of the newcomers were children much too young to work, and they were occupying a home really intended for working boys. It was obviously time to take counsel with St. Joseph.

Although there was now much less uncertainty about going ahead with new expenditures, still to raise funds for such an undertaking would necessitate a drive of some kind. He knew that an appeal to the members of the Union would not be made in vain. By 1881 they had spread over the earth, and the promoters were seemingly never idle, to judge from the overwhelming amount of mail that came daily to Box 3502.

Of course, as was usual with Father Drumgoole's plans, they went beyond the immediate necessity. Such a home in the country for the little children would perhaps have a wider use later. It could be made not only into a home and school for children, but might enable him to carry out still another dream: a vocational school which, when a boy was old enough, would equip him with a trade.

First of all, he must seek a good location for this country home. So, with the faithful Mr. Dougherty beside him, he began looking at possible sites. Some properties proved far too expensive; some completely unsuited to his purposes. It was clear that it would be difficult to find exactly what he wanted for what he could afford to pay.

On one trip of exploration the two men had seen an estate which at first sight seemed to be exactly right. They had taken the long trip by horsecar and train, and finally by horse and wagon, to the Halliday mansion in Westchester County. It stood on 700 acres, some of it good farm land, a great deal of it wooded. The garrulous old caretaker who showed it to them said it had been bought by a bank at foreclosure for $50,000.

The house was of stone and so were the large stables; there was even a little stone chapel. From the outside it looked very promising, but when they went inside and saw the great hall and the other rooms, they were disappointed. The interior was still all unfinished. It was clear that no one had ever lived there.

"Someone's folly," said Mr. Dougherty forthrightly, "and evidently copied from an expensive European model."

Despite the unfinished condition of the house, Father Drumgoole looked at it with longing eyes. It would be a wonderful place for his children, he knew. But he realized that it would be an impossible choice: the cost of making it habitable would be at least as much as the purchase price. He turned away sadly from the alluring stone buildings.

Several promising New Jersey prospects turned out to be equally disappointing. One on Long Island was excellent for his purposes, but it was priced at the impossible sum of $125,000.

One day in late April of 1882 the two men went to

Staten Island. The Bennett farm at Pleasant Plains, far out on the island, had been suggested earlier as a possible site, but at this point Father Drumgoole was discouraged, and besides not too optimistic about such an out-of-the-way place. However, as he had been promising himself a one-day holiday he thought he would combine business and pleasure by a visit to the Bennett farm.

The holiday began with a fine dinner of roast goose and apple dumplings, with Mr. Dougherty as host. Then the two took the ferry to Staten Island and the horsecars to West Brighton. They went to call first on the Sisters of Charity at their school. There Father Drumgoole gave a short talk to the children, partook of refreshments of milk and poundcake, and then, unfortunately—so thought his companion—got into such an interesting conversation with Sister Raphael on school problems that they all but missed the cars for New Brighton where another call had to be made on the Sisters at St. Peter's school.

By this time the day was all but gone, and they had to forego the visit to the Bennett farm, to Mr. Dougherty's deep annoyance. Not until nine o'clock that night did they reach the New York ferry.

Since the day had been spent without a glimpse of their objective, the two went again to Staten Island a few weeks later. This time Mr. Dougherty saw to it that they made no visits on the way.

At Tottenville they rented a boat and rode along the shore, as the boatman pointed out to them the farms for sale along the way. He knew about the Bennett farm, too. "The old lady wants to sell because she's all alone with her granddaughter," he said. "I can put you ashore there if you like."

They found no one at home in the pleasant farmhouse,

but Father Drumgoole liked the wide fields, the water boundary, the good air that blew in from the ocean, the sunny beach. Opposite were the Highlands of Navesink, and in full view he saw an ocean liner passing the Narrows on its way to foreign ports. A farm like this would not only bring health to his children but perhaps here some of them could learn to be farmers. And then, remembering the little children sent West against their parents' will, he thought how fine it would be if these boys could go West someday, too, not as helpless children but as trained and efficient young men.

Dougherty found in his pocket an old business envelope and on this Father Drumgoole penciled a few words: If Mrs. Bennett wanted to talk with him about selling her farm, would she call on the writer at his New York address?

Before he went further with this project, however, he busied himself with settling another and a more urgent need. The helpers he had employed at the Mission were efficient, and the volunteer helpers a great and useful aid, but it was growing increasingly clear that he also needed a united corps that would work as a team. Such a team, and at its best, was to be found only in a congregation of religious. With them on his staff he would not have a succession of workers who came and went, but a permanent group who would make the Mission their home.

Several years before, when Father Drumgoole had been in Buffalo to attend the funeral of Father Rice of Our Lady of Angels' Seminary, he had called at the Franciscan convent to visit a cousin of his who was a religious there. He had asked her about their work and learned that this group, a part of the great Franciscan family, were teachers, nurses, and visitors in the homes of the poor.

The congregation had been founded in 1855 by Bishop Neumann of Philadelphia, who, on a visit to Rome, had been granted permission to found a community of Sisters in his diocese. Pius IX, himself a Franciscan tertiary, had suggested that such a group adopt the Franciscan rule and the bishop had agreed. When, on his return to the United States, three women came to see him, saying they wished to consecrate themselves to God, and they wanted especially to work under the rule of St. Francis, it seemed a direct answer to prayer. He started his new community with these three women.

He wrote their rule himself. They were to unite the active life with that of prayer; their principal work was the care of the sick whom they visited in their homes. Later, as postulants became more numerous, the little congregation began to devote itself to its secondary work— that of the education of children.

In 1860 this community had opened a second house in Buffalo in order to provide a home for the aged and infirm. In 1862 the Buffalo house separated from that in Philadelphia and by 1880 this new group had nine houses in the diocese of Buffalo.

Father Drumgoole, remembering these Sisters and their work, wondered if he could prevail upon the superior of this community to send some of its members to him. In order to strengthen his request he went first to see his friend Bishop Ryan of Buffalo and ended by placing the entire matter in his hands.

"Long ago they promised me at the motherhouse that when my Mission was ready they would come to help me care for my children," he told the Bishop. That prelate, although he had really not enough Sisters for his own needs, could not refuse his help in so urgent a need. So together they went to the convent to consult the superior, with the result that Father Drumgoole returned to New York with the promise of Sisters to staff his Mission. The New York archdiocesan office willingly gave its approval and wrote the superior that all necessary permissions for the observation of their rule would be forthcoming.

On July 2, 1882, six Sisters came to the Mission of the Immaculate Virgin with Sister Bonaventure as their superior. And before a week had passed Father Drumgoole knew that this was what he had long needed. Now he had workers who would remain with him, women who were devoted to children, and who could understand his aims. They not only assisted him in the running of the Mission, but they also taught religion to the children. To the children in his Mission St. Joseph and he had given a father's care. Now the Sisters would give them the love of a mother.

In June 1882 Father Drumgoole bought from Mrs. Bennett the 138 acres of farm, with all its stock, crops, and farming implements for $22,000. This included 2,000 feet of shore along the bluff of Prince's Bay.

A survey was made at once in order to find out how soon, after putting up a few additional buildings, the place could be made habitable for some of the children. For he hoped that very summer to bring to Staten Island the little ones from the nursery at Fort Washington, as well as the smaller and more delicate boys from the city Mission.

Meantime, in order to insure grounds large enough for future needs, he bought an adjoining farm of seventy acres for $15,000. These negotiations were much more difficult than had been those with Mrs. Bennett. When Father Drumgoole and Mr. Dougherty went to discuss the matter with the owner of the farm, a Mr. Jessup, they found him working his fields, chewing vigorously as he hoed his rows of corn.

"Pretty old for such hard work, aren't you?" asked Father Drumgoole kindly.

The old man straightened up and spat tobacco juice from the corner of his mouth. "Eighty-four years old," he said briefly. Then, with a hard look at his questioner, he added, "And I still got all my wits about me. I'm clear as a bell."

This was obviously said in order to discourage any attempt to bring down the asking price on the farm, which was just what the visitors had been hoping to do. When they suggested a lower figure, the old man simply shook his head and went back to his hoeing. "If you think it's too high, you keep your money and I'll keep my farm," he said shortly and decisively. It was eventually bought on Mr. Jessup's own terms, for the land was needed and would be of great value for many reasons including drainage.

In the same month Father Drumgoole bought the small Nance farm which bordered the Jessup land for $5,000. When these papers had been signed, over a cup of tea, Mrs. Nance presented Father Drumgoole with a package of fourteen fresh eggs for the boys at the Mission, for she had listened to the story of his work with sympathetic interest.

The best house on the group of farms was on the Bennett land, a two-story frame structure with a wide porch. Not far from it Father Drumgoole planned to build several new frame houses—a main building with a chapel, another with classrooms and dormitories, and a third for a laundry and to provide living quarters for the women to be employed for domestic work. He hoped soon to have a good dairy and a fine chicken yard and had already hired Mr. Murphy, an experienced farmer, to take charge.

The others were too busy at first to bother with the history of the newly acquired properties, but Mr. Dougherty, always interested in ancient landmarks, began to look up the background of some of theirs. He learned that these farms were part of a great tract of pre-Revolutionary days and when he delved deeper he came up with much interesting information.

Staten Island for centuries had been a populous place. In the sixteenth century it had been settled by the French, then had come the Dutch, the English, the Germans, and long before any of them, the Indians had fished its waters and hunted its woods and planted its fields. The earliest white men to come there were seeking a short cut to the Indies and its gold, and reached the island by accident, remaining to establish a vast trade in furs. After the Dutch the British took over and called it the Shire of Yorkshire. "It was a modest tract," Mr. Dougherty commented, "that took in Staten Island, Westchester, and Long Island."

When, in 1675, the tract was divided, a certain Captain Christopher Billopp received from the crown some 1,300 acres of the shire on Staten Island. During the Revolution the Billopps were strongly King's men as were most of their neighbors. George Washington himself said of Staten Island that its inhabitants had "shown themselves our most inveterate enemies." When Lord Howe arrived, the Staten Islanders had welcomed him with a huge bonfire in which they dumped quantities of continental paper money.

It was at the Billopp home in 1776 that an unsuccessful peace conference took place between General Howe, Benjamin Franklin, and John Adams. The latter wrote in his diary that he found the Billopp home in a very poor state, though he admired the fine living-room rug. On that occasion he greatly resented, and made note of, the battalion of Hessians—"looking fierce as the Furies and with bayonets fixed, which we neither understood nor required."

After the failure of the conference the war went on. In 1778 Lord Howe went home and Clinton took command. That same year Captain Billopp was captured, thanks to a patriotic lady whom he thought a good loyalist. Not until late in 1787 did the last of the British army leave Staten Island, two months after the surrender at Yorktown. Christopher Billopp was freed and went to Canada; the family property was considered forfeit, divided into smaller parcels, and sold.

"There's history here and plenty of it," said Mr. Dougherty to the amused Father Drumgoole, "and your farms are sitting right in the middle of it."

One day Father Drumgoole, after a busy day at the Staten Island property, came back to the City House—as they began to call it now—to find a reporter waiting for an interview on the new venture.

Father Drumgoole described it briefly and added, "We are going to raise corn, wheat, potatoes, and vegetables. We now own thirty-five cows and some good horses and 300 chickens."

"You sound like a regular farmer," said the reporter.

Father Drumgoole smiled and then looked sober. "We city people will never be that, I am afraid, but we'll do our best. And so far we have been fortunate. Blessings have attended our labors and all is going well. But of course," he added hastily, "that is due to St. Joseph whom we have to thank for it all."

The reporter went away looking somewhat baffled by this pious statement. He wrote that Father Drumgoole was like the man in the East who rubbed a lamp and a genie appeared to build him a palace; Father Drumgoole had rubbed his little statue of St. Joseph and lo, a fine structure had appeared for the little Arabs of the city streets.

It was very true that there were times when his success troubled Father Drumgoole; this was the reason he had looked so serious when he answered the reporter as he had. For that very day an admiring visitor had said to him, "I don't know how you do it—lodge hundreds of boys, build at an estimated cost of $300,000, and all paid for—no mortgages, no bonds, no loans—and now this big farm property."

This was not the first time such a statement had been made to Father Drumgoole, so evidently intended as a compliment to his own ability. "Nor do I," he had said solemnly to his visitor, "and it bothers me sometimes. But I comfort myself by saying that God chooses His instruments where He wishes. They are sometimes very weak vessels and it is really only He who enables a man to do anything."

In September 1883, on the feast of Our Lady's Nativity, the boys from the City House arrived for a visit at the new farm; they represented a vanguard of the army to come later. Most of them had never made this trip to the island before, and on the ferry their admiring glances were divided equally between the city they were leaving and the green country they were approaching.

After the ride down the island, as they approached Tottenville, they saw first Red Bank Lighthouse, flying the stars and stripes in the bright morning sunlight. Then the newly-built tower and the cross that topped it came in view. And they knew they were at home.

The day had been chosen for the blessing of the new Chapel of St. Anne and for the confirmation of 200 boys from the City House. Archbishop Corrigan presided and afterward gave a talk in which he spoke of the completely new way of life which Christianity had brought into the world. Rome and Greece had had no works of mercy for their poor or their friendless; no thought of charity was in their hearts, no word for it in their vocabularies. In the whole ancient world there was no hospital or asylum; the weak child was often left to perish. In surprise the pagans, seeing what the Christians did for their sick and poor and helpless, had been wont to say, "See how these Christians love one another."

The Archbishop was taken on a tour of the grounds where, although nothing was as yet fully completed, the plan of the work was now clear. He admired the fine kitchen, the wide airy corridors, the well-lighted dormitories. Father Drumgoole told him that he and his architects had studied the plans of the best institutions in the country and had added to them some ideas of their own. There were now eight new frame buildings and a perfect network of lightning rods on top of them. The fields of grain lay golden in the sun; the herd of cows grazed contentedly under the trees; the long runs were filled with chickens.

"We want everything to be the best," said Father Drumgoole earnestly, as he paced along beside the Archbishop, "for a boy's surroundings of poverty and want are often the cause of his later crimes. And all of the boys will help here. The little ones can bring in water and sweep, fold clothes, gather potatoes. In an emergency I can have some of the big boys from the city come down to help. I wish I could have more of these older ones here now to do what the few already here are doing—learning to make clothing and shoes. For it is my intention as soon as possible to open a training school for other trades in addition to farming."

"Have you named your country home as yet?" asked the Archbishop.

"Indeed I have, Your Excellency. I named it years ago really—even before I was ordained." And he told the interested prelate of the Sisters near the seminary at Niagara who had been so kind to him. "I have always intended, if I ever built a home for children in the country, to call it Mount Loretto."

On his way back to New York the Archbishop talked with the young priests who had come with him about Father John—of his small beginnings, of the real home he had made of the first rundown and poorly equipped warehouse, of the school he opened where a boy could learn to earn a livelihood, of the later great skyscraper building raised through his efforts, as was this new home in the wide countryside.

"He has accomplished a great deal already, but when he opens his vocational school he will have accomplished perhaps the greatest good of all," said the Archbishop.

He was no doubt right, for he knew the conditions of the great city. But he knew also that for the little children the greatest benefit that could be given was the lovely country and the wide waters, a place for them to grow up healthy and happy, no longer waifs of a careless city but the loved and wanted children of the trio who watched over them—Our Lady, St. Joseph, and Father John.

The boys from the City House had had such a wonderful day that Father Drumgoole was sorry that they must leave the country when evening came. He had watched their unalloyed delight in what was for many of them the first day they had ever spent in the country, and saw how they had enjoyed the freedom of the orchards and the beaches. He felt it was a pity to have them leave this green place and go back to the dirt and squalor of the city. Soon, he promised himself, they could come here for longer stays, so that the flush from the warm sun which was now on their faces would become that of a season and not merely of a day.

The first visitors to the farm were chiefly from the city, but after a while local people began to show an interest in the venture in their midst. The older farmers had not liked the proximity of a Catholic institution and especially did not relish the idea of hordes of children roaming over their fields and orchards. But as the boys stayed on their own property, the farmers grew less fearful. On the occasion when the Archbishop came to bless the new Mount Loretto many Staten Island people had been present. In fact, an old-timer told Father Drumgoole that it was the largest gathering he had ever seen on the island. The people had been not only curious but friendly, and Father Drumgoole was happy to feel he and his were being accepted.

One troublesome matter which came up shortly was that of the oyster growing rights, of which Father Drumgoole had never heard until the neighbors began coming to him with protests. A surveyor had gone over the property which was under water to settle the riparian rights of Mount Loretto. The survey showed that they had 255 acres in all, according to Mr. Sylvester, the government surveyor, but the residents of farms in the neighborhood were opposed to allowing him to use the waters beside the farm since it might destroy their oyster industry.

In fact, one man came to explain to the amazed and bewildered Father Drumgoole that he had a bed planted right in front of the Bennett property and that if any young varmints went swimming there, there was no telling what might happen to the growing oysters. The matter was settled pacifically by an agreement that oyster growers were to have the underwater rights until the several years it would take the very youngest oysters to mature and be marketed.

All that summer, whenever Father Drumgoole could manage it, boys from the City House were brought out to the farm, and swam and played to their hearts' content. Raritan Bay made for fine swimming, and Father Drumgoole had procured a large floating bathhouse which could accommodate more than fifty children at a time and which they used in relays. Once the choir boys came out for the day and sang all Father Drumgoole's favorite songs for him.

At Thanksgiving everyone came down, including all the children from the Fort Washington nursery. Those from the City House had paraded from Broadway to South Ferry, with their band playing all the way. As, after their journey they drew near the main house at Mount Loretto, they signaled their coming by the strains of the "Star-Spangled Banner." Eight hundred sat down to the well-filled tables that day. And just as had always been the custom at the City House, here, too, the poor came and were fed and made welcome.

That evening the whole pattern of things changed. Of the many who had come to the farm to spend Thanksgiving only 200 returned to the city. The younger ones, including all the Fort Washington boys and some of the Sisters, remained at Mount Loretto. This would now be their permanent home. The dormitories were ready. School was to open the following week.

This change had many advantages, one of them the fact that it would leave more room for the girls who had been at Fort Washington and would remain there for a time. But only for a time. Father Drumgoole hoped before long to transfer to Mount Loretto especially the girls who had brothers there, in keeping with his firm conviction that families should, as much as possible, be kept together.

That Christmas of 1883 there were two celebrations for Father Drumgoole's children. At Mount Loretto more than 400 received Communion and more than that in the City House. This year the cost of the Christmas celebration was very high because there were two Homes and two sets of children. But this was the kind of financial hurdle that had never proved difficult for Father Drumgoole. Each year the costs were completely met by one friend or another—by the Leavy family, a member of whom had given the money for the very first celebration at Warren Street; by Charles Peyton, the seminarian at Rome; and in later years by a man whose son, a priest, had died young and who made this form of charity his memorial to him.

The poor who came for Christmas dinner at the City House that year was large and gathered early, evidently seeking warmth as well as food. A reporter, come for a story on the boys' celebration, asked in surprise how many outsiders had been invited.

"Oh, they all have a standing invitation," said Father Drumgoole, evidently undaunted by their numbers. "We give a meal to anyone who can't get a dinner elsewhere. They are God's poor and we ask them to come here in His name."

What especially pleased Father Drumgoole that Christmas day was the visit of an old friend. Father Landry had come down from Our Lady of Angels' Seminary, and in his talk at the City House he praised everything he saw—the Mission, the priests, the Sisters, the children. Of the last he said, after he had seen the performance of their Christmas play, "I never met children in an institution before who took part in a play as well as they did, and as for their singing, they go at it as if they had had years of experience under fine masters." And Father Drumgoole listened to this praise with all the delight of a real parent in his fine household.

The winter was very cold, and in the City House many people came to be fed each day—from fifty to 300. There were the sick to whom food must be taken. And Father Drumgoole always gave his Sisters money to take to certain people whose sensitiveness made them unwilling to let others know of their need.

Once when he came to the City House on a cold snowy morning he met an old man who made apologies for his presence. "I told the Sister right in the beginning that I wasn't a Catholic," he said, "but she said it didn't matter. And I tell you, Mister, that this meal they give me every day has saved me from starving this winter."

By the end of 1883 there were 600 children in the Staten Island Mission. The school had seven trained teachers and gave both classical and commercial courses. More land had been bought: the Vail farm and the Seguine farm —both with good houses on them. It seemed to Father Drumgoole that for a time at least he would have room for every child sent to him. And it was with a grateful heart that he repeated daily with his children at the City House and at Mount Loretto the prayer now known to them all as St. Joseph's Union prayer.

He had written it himself earlier in the year, asking the approval of Rome for its recitation and also a blessing on his work. He had made this request early in February, hoping he would not have to wait too many months for a reply, but the answer had come quickly. After Mass on St. Joseph's Day he noticed that one letter in his mail bore a Roman postmark. He opened it with not the least thought of what its contents might be, and was overcome to find it was from the Holy See. Pope Leo XIII had granted an indulgence of 400 days to all members of the Union who recited twice daily the brief prayer Father Drumgoole had himself suggested and 200 days to those who recited it once a day. The words were exactly as he had written them:

> "Most Holy and Immaculate Mother of God and
> glorious St. Joseph, Guardians and patrons
> of our House and Union, intercede for us, your
> devoted children, now and at the hour of our
> death. Amen."

He had prayed hard for the approval of this prayer and for this indulgence, and it had come to him on St. Joseph's own feast day!

⟫⟫-⟫⟫

13

Father of Two Homes

By 1884 there were 900 children in the two homes. The Society for the Prevention of Cruelty to Children had sent Father Drumgoole 200 of them, nearly as many as they sent to the Catholic Protectory. The city grant, made because the Mission "gratuitously aids, supports, and assists the poor," was a considerable help to him. In 1884 this amounted to $4,000, and the sum increased with each year; before long the Mission was receiving the second highest amount paid to any religious institution in the city.

Even so, the Mission managed to give as well as receive. In addition to feeding and clothing the poor at home, stipends were sent for Masses to missionary priests; help was given to a scheme for placing destitute Irish families on farm land in Western states, and a sum was sent to Ireland as a contribution to famine relief.

Our Lady's birthday was always an important feast for the Mission of the Immaculate Virgin. On that day in 1879 the foundation stone of the house on Lafayette Street had been blessed; and in 1882 the chapel at Mount Loretto. As 1884 was the nineteen hundredth anniversary of the feast, Mount Loretto planned to celebrate.

In the City House Our Lady's statue was placed in the sanctuary and Father Drumgoole led a procession in her honor. In the afternoon everyone—all the children and all the employees—went to Staten Island by boat and were welcomed at the landing by the Citizens' Cornet Band. After the train ride to Tottenville everybody walked the short distance from the railway station to the house over a wooden path which Father Drumgoole had had laid for visitors and which was much shorter than the winding carriage road. It was a very warm day, but the great trees shaded the marchers all the way.

Later that afternoon there was a procession of the Blessed Sacrament. Father Drumgoole, pacing slowly under a beautiful new canopy finished by the Sisters only the night before, carried the Host. The procession marched from the chapel under arches of evergreen decked with flowers, and some fifty of the smallest children, all in white, walked ahead strewing flowers in the path of Our Lord. Three temporary altars had been erected on the green lawns, each flower-laden, each shaped like a heart, and there the Triple Benediction was given.

The day was noisy and happy as well as sunny and very hot. Only a few sails crept up the bay, and no leaf stirred. But the boys raced up and down all day, evidently not minding the heat at all.

Father Drumgoole had told the assembled children, "You may amuse yourselves till dinnertime." The polite silence with which they were waiting to hear an expected sermon was immediately broken and they scattered in all directions, some to the shore, some to the woods, like birds out of a cage.

At Thanksgiving the City House boys came again to the country and after a wonderful dinner Father Drumgoole made his customary patriotic address, speaking to them of liberty under God and the necessity of never forgetting that all liberty came from Him. "It is the glory of every American citizen," he told them solemnly, "that by his vote he has the right to help preserve that hard-won liberty." And then he spoke, as he so often did, of the fact that to be a good Catholic meant that one was also a good American. "Read the history of the United States," he said. "It will make you feel that same spirit of patriotism, and when you grow up and vote then you can use that vote to uphold the honor of your country. This is true patriotism, to defend your land either with your life in war or your vote in peace. And if anyone tells you that Catholics cannot be good Americans tell them to read their history books—about Carroll risking his fortune to sign the Declaration of Independence, Hughes and his embassy to Europe, Sheridan leading our armies. But," and the voice grew very solemn, "always remember that the man who barters his vote is a traitor to his land, as much so as a spy in war."

By 1885 Father Drumgoole gave these figures to the members of the Union by way of *The Homeless Child:* 16,000 children cared for; 5,000 prepared for First Communion, one half of whom had been cared for during the entire year free; 6,000 poor people given free clothing. In addition many families whose breadwinner was ill had been cared for temporarily and thousands fed at the two homes.

When in 1882 Cardinal McCloskey had dedicated the chapel in the new Home on Lafayette Street, he had said it might be the last public act of that kind which he would be able to perform, and so it turned out. Not long before his death in 1885 he sent for Father Drumgoole. When the latter came to Mount St. Vincent he was saddened to see how tired the old prelate looked, how ill he evidently was.

The Cardinal wanted to see Father Drumgoole for a very special reason.

"I do not expect to see the end God has in view for your plan or to see it completed," he told him, "but I hope you will be able to carry it out faithfully as you once outlined it to me. Much has been done, I know, but I want to hear more about the occupational work. How is that coming along?"

Nothing could make Father Drumgoole happier than to talk about this cherished subject. "I am leaving nothing undone, Your Eminence, to bring that about," he assured the prelate. "At the farm my plans in this regard are being completed, at least in one respect. I am ready to put up one building entirely for boys interested in agriculture, and I shall have competent men to teach them all that goes with good farming. Already some of the boys who are helping Mr. Murphy tell me they want to become farmers. And I shall give them wages and have them save some of it, and perhaps when they are grown they will have enough for a down payment on a farm of their own."

The Cardinal nodded his satisfaction. "And how about the others, those who don't care for farming as a trade?"

"Those who want to go into business go, when they are old enough, to the City House. Every kind of commercial work is being taught there at present. But what I plan to establish very soon are trade schools at Mount Loretto, and we are working on these plans now. It will cost a great deal of money and so I must move slowly. First of all, we must have a church there."

"And the money?" asked the Cardinal.

"St. Joseph will provide it, Your Eminence," he answered simply, and the Cardinal, with equal simplicity, said, "Of course he will."

Before he left Father Drumgoole told the Cardinal how grateful he was for the excellent young priests who had been sent him as assistants, both for the City House and Mount Loretto—Father Degnan for the first and young Father McNichol for the second.

Early in 1885 Father Drumgoole learned of a widowed father in the nearby little town of Krieserville who was unable to take proper care of his family. The oldest, a girl of twelve, was not up to the task of running the home, and Father Drumgoole offered to take them. The boys went to the boys' house dormitory, the little girls remained with the Sisters. They had been at Mount Loretto only a short time when their father gave permission to have them all baptized.

Perhaps it was this sudden intrusion of girls into a home hitherto housing only boys which brought about another change. Quarters were at last arranged at Mount Loretto for the girls still at Fort Washington. They were brought to the island and placed in an addition to the house built behind the chapel wing. And now, when word went out that Mount Loretto had received girls, shelter was asked for more, and by 1886 the "Female Department" was completed.

Often in the evening the girls, tucked in their beds in the little dormitory, could hear Sister Agnes and Sister Angela singing such songs as "Dear Little Shamrock," and they knew that Father Drumgoole had come in for his brief evening call on the Sisters and had asked them for one of his favorite songs. A little later, when he went through the dormitory, heads would pop up from pillows and voices chorus, "Goodnight, Father." "God bless you all," he would answer, as he made the sign of the cross over them.

Father Drumgoole was to become very proud of his girls, who proved themselves fine students. When he examined their monthly reports, he was gratified to find many eighties, and among the older girls some grades high in the nineties.

Best of all, now the children of one family could see each other occasionally and so preserve their unity. "If the boys have sisters, how can we bear to separate them?" he used to ask, or "Shall we allow these poor little girls to be sent elsewhere because we will not take them?" Now such questions were answered.

At first he could take only a small group of girls; the next year, in a house on the Bennett property, he was able to take many more. But when that time came, poor Sister Gonzaga, in charge of the girls' department, was greatly overworked and Sister Angela was sent to help her, and a little later Sister Clare.

One summer day Father Drumgoole had planned a wonderful trip on the magnificent new steamer *Grand Republic,* which had been chartered for the occasion. For days before the boys talked excitedly on this one topic. Father Drumgoole was as thrilled as they and, like a professional guide, described to them the wonderful ship and the places they would see. The eve of the event arrived and no one—except perhaps a worried Father Drumgoole—noticed a cold wind blowing from the east.

Next morning dawned bleak and gray and a slanting rain beat against the windows. Some of the boys held St. Benedict medals hopefully against the wet panes; some scanned the leaden skies with anxious eyes, seeking for a comforting bit of blue. Then Father Drumgoole came into the main play hall where most of them were congregated.

It was a bad moment for him, too, as all eyes turned to the one person who could surely do something about it.

He did not fail them. He climbed a chair so that everyone could see and hear him. "Boys, I sent early this morning to the City House for the band. We are going to have a grand party right now and right here!"

He gave a signal, and the band, which had been waiting in the corridor, burst into loud music as its members, gay in their uniforms, marched in. Father Drumgoole assumed the role of drum major, led the band through the room, using his walking stick as baton. Hundreds of boys fell in step behind the band, their unhappiness forgotten in this present happy activity. Through the connected buildings wound the procession, and finally the march became a riotous game of follow the leader, where each boy did his best to get ahead of the rest in emulating and exaggerating Father Drumgoole's lead.

When the procession reached the long dining room, they marched in single file around the long tables to the tune of "Pop Goes the Weasel." Then Father Drumgoole called a halt and the boys looked hungrily at the laden tables.

Outside, the rain continued to beat against the windowpanes. The *Grand Republic* was no doubt anchored at her pier. But inside the Mission the happy horde sang gay songs and ate a mountain of ice cream and cake. The day was saved.

Father Drumgoole had met only a few Catholic families on Staten Island when he first arrived, but among them were the De Comeaus, who were very wealthy and very generous with their help to the Mission. The mother and two daughters were devoted to their Church, but the father had long ago left it and despite their pleading refused to return. However, he was a good friend of Father Drumgoole and the latter spent pleasant hours in the De Comeau mansion. There was an understanding that religion must not be mentioned unless Mr. de Comeau himself spoke of it. Father Drumgoole agreed to this, though reluctantly. More than once Archbishop Corrigan, who had succeeded Cardinal McCloskey, and who was devoted to the old gentleman, asked Father Drumgoole about the state of Mr. de Comeau's soul. So far the answer had not been reassuring.

Now in February of 1885 one of the daughters, Yolande, sent word to Father Drumgoole in New York that her father was not only very ill but sinking rapidly. As soon as Father Drumgoole reached the island he hastened to visit the old gentleman.

Yolande met him at the door, looking very sad and troubled. "Father wants to see you, but asked me to warn you that he is not prepared for confession and you are not to mention the subject if you go in to talk with him. He says when he is ready he will tell you."

Father Drumgoole nodded as if in agreement, but he decided privately to act as seemed best. Learning Mr. de Comeau had fallen asleep, he put off the visit and promised to come later in the day. When he reached the house the second time, it was to learn that Mr. de Comeau had suffered a relapse. When he went to the sick man's bedside, the latter made an effort to smile when he recognized his visitor. Then his expression grew defiant. "Did my daughter give you my message?" he whispered.

Father Drumgoole nodded. "But I've come to settle the question right now for good. Once you told me there was no one in whom you placed more confidence than in me. Now I've come to test it."

The voice was a little stronger. "I'm not ready and I won't do it till I am."

"But why are you not ready? We've talked about this before. It was different then, but by this time tomorrow you may be in eternity, man, and you'll never get to heaven without a good confession. You must know there is no time to lose."

The eyes remained obstinate. "I can't and I won't," he said.

Father Drumgoole smiled at his old friend. "Well, suppose I tell you that I have a message from God for you and hereby am delivering it through St. Joseph." He did not wait for further objections, but put on his stole. "Come, prove that you have more confidence in me than in anyone, priest or layman, as you told me more than once. Why don't you make a confidant of me? Tell me what is the matter and then make your confession or not as you please."

This persuasive talk evidently disarmed the old gentleman. He sighed and smiled wryly. "All right, Father John, you win."

After the sick man had given his whole story, he was spent from talking and remained silent for a few minutes. Then he smiled. "And now you've won and I shall no longer be on the side of Lucifer."

He asked to have Yolande called, and when she came in rather timidly and saw her father's face she went to him quickly and took his hand in hers. And so Father Drumgoole left them after promising to say a Mass of thanksgiving next morning, asking them to unite their intentions with his. As soon as he reached home he wrote a long letter to Archbishop Corrigan to tell him that the old gentleman's obstinate refusal to be reconciled with his Church was ended.

At the end of his letter he added, "He is such a good, kindhearted old gentleman that it would be a pity if he had dropped off unprepared to meet his God."

Mr. de Comeau died a few days later, and after his funeral his daughter Yolande went to see Father Drumgoole. She wanted to do something, she said, to show her gratitude. She would like, if it were possible, to build a home for the care of orphaned blind girls for whom there was no place in a Catholic institution. She offered to give $100,000 for the work.

Within the same year Mrs. de Comeau also passed away, and Yolande asked if both her parents might be buried in the little Mount Loretto cemetery. Father Drumgoole agreed. Then she told him of her own intention, now that she had no further responsibilities: she wanted to give her life wholly to God. She planned to become a religious.

Father Drumgoole knew that this was no sudden decision. From childhood she had wanted to be a religious but her parents had opposed it. When Father Drumgoole had first come to Staten Island she had found in him a friend and counsellor and to him she had told her hopes. Even the desire to found a home for blind girls was no sudden impulse. Some years before she had found that the sound of her voice greatly attracted a lonely blind child in the neighborhood, and from contact with this child came her interest in others, and a resolve someday to devote her life to the blind.

By 1887 the number of children in the two homes had increased to 1,300. In the City House there were now fewer newsboys or bootblacks or sweeps—many of them were employed in banks and stores. They also became hatters, butchers, masons, truck drivers, tailors, and some few qualified as schoolteachers. Some passed their Civil Service examinations by studying at the evening school. Some were in the armed forces. The department stores—A. T. Stewart and Lord & Taylor among them—were always ready to employ boys from the Mission.

The doctors who visited the Mission—for a new law ordered a monthly examination of all children cared for in an institution—gave it an excellent rating. Deaths had always been rare; those that did occur were usually due to the fact that some children arrived in very poor condition. In a year when measles were very prevalent, the Mission had not a single case. There was not, and had not been for a long time, a single case of the common disease of the day among the poor—sore eyes.

Even though Mr. Letchworth had a few years before given high praise to the Mission, certain city authorities were critical of the methods of Father Drumgoole's Home. In 1886 Mrs. Josephine Lowell, one of the commissioners, reported that she was appalled by the situation there. "He has no active management and only eleven 'Sisters,' " she wrote of the City House, "and the management is left chiefly to hired men in both his institutions. I consider it a great evil."

She had evidently come to grips with Father Drumgoole personally, for later her report bore the added tart comment: "I am sorry to say he considers me as something worse than a heathen because I do not think religious training of the children more than offsets the want of proper education in other directions."

The chief point of her irritation no doubt was that

Father Drumgoole received considerable funds from the city for his institution—$96,000 in 1885—yet was insisting on running it his own way. There was, she said, no "manual training," but the fact was that the plans were all but ready even then to carry out this, his own great dream.

But he could—and perhaps did—point out to Mrs. Lowell such advanced features as the grouping of children by age and ability; in most institutions of the day children were thrown together with little regard for these. In his homes there were two divisions—one, those too young to work; the other, those who were wage earners or apprentices. He could point also to the scholarships he was receiving for his more gifted students. But then, even as far back as 1879, he had insisted that his boys must have a grammar-school education before they looked for work—an extremely radical idea.

It was difficult to get the annoyed Mrs. Lowell to listen to such statements. In her opinion "the present object seems to be to collect the greatest number possible and maintain them at the expense of private charity and public money and educate them to be good Catholics." She saw the work only with the eye of sectarian prejudice; saw that the methods were not those of the organization in which she was trained, and said that "as a means for the education of future citizens of New York, it is a sad thing to contemplate."

However, despite this criticism, the work went on and in Father Drumgoole's own way. The children were healthy and he could point to the few deaths and the rare illnesses. He reunited families when it was possible; he had a staff of five teachers. His boys were getting good jobs as they grew up. In fact, his methods would seem to later observers to have been modern and often ahead of his time.

And he had added one ingredient often lacked by public institutions: the love of a devoted father for his children. His work had begun on this personal basis; he could never have made it impersonal no matter how large it grew. His one crime in the eyes of people like Mrs. Lowell was his difference in approach. To him these were children of God (and of the Catholic Church, Mrs. Lowell might have added sharply) as well as future citizens of New York. And to him the idea of a family was always paramount. Joseph, Mary, and the Child were the ideal family. So, first of all, the family must, if possible, be held together to protect the child. If that proved impossible, he and the Mission must be father and mother to him. The rest—education, trades, and so on—followed. But they did not come first. First came love, and that meant the inculcating of faith in the protecting love of God.

That year Father Drumgoole lost a faithful assistant at Mount Loretto. Father Degnan was appointed to the pastorship of St. Mary's Church. It was a sorrow to lose him, but Father Drumgoole took comfort in the thought that Father Degnan would be going to a place he had regarded for many years as his own spiritual home. Young Father McNichol was now placed in charge of the City House.

As for Father Drumgoole, he divided his time fairly evenly between the two houses. He loved both Homes and both sets of children, but there was little doubt that his real delight was to be at Mount Loretto. And there was even less doubt of his welcome there.

When his square figure in the big black cloak was seen coming up the steps the children swarmed to meet him, clutching his hands, trying to climb to his shoulders, and many tried to get under the big circular cape he wore. No child was pushed away no matter how tired Father John was. For all there was the welcome word, the personal greeting, for he knew every child.

On the Staten Island ferry he was, of course, very well known, and many smiled at him when they saw him sitting by himself on the upper deck, the wind on his face, his eyes seemingly looking into the distance and seeing no one. Those familiar with him knew what he was doing: he was reciting his rosary and holding it out of sight in the folds of his big cloak.

On one occasion a woman who did not know him hurried to one of the boat officials, saying there was a man with a snake on board. Investigation showed it was merely Father Drumgoole and the snake was the big black rosary which now and then escaped from the confines of his cloak.

To him this brief ride on the water was his one opportunity, save his Mass, when he could be alone and without interruption. But even that was beginning to be difficult. Everywhere he was greeted, for he and his Mission and his children were now accepted as a part of the island.

When he first came to Mount Loretto there had been, so far as he knew, only one Catholic family within three miles. The rest, principally Huguenot descendants of the immigrants who fled there after the revocation of the Edict of Nantes, were now his friends. At first they had resented the coming of the Catholics, now there were converts among them. Within a year fifteen persons had been confirmed, along with the children from the Mission.

Many of the neighbors at Staten Island said that, though they had often heard of miracles, they had never seen one until they saw Mount Loretto. Father Drumgoole did not phrase it like that. He would no doubt have preferred to call it the result of the long and unceasing labor of his patron St. Joseph in behalf of homeless children.

"We have built thirteen houses here in these few years," he wrote in *The Homeless Child* in 1887, "or perhaps it would be better if I said St. Joseph has built them."

Of late he had been carrying on considerable correspondence with Rome regarding the plans for a church he intended to build at Mount Loretto. Cardinal Parocchi, Vicar General of Rome, had showed much interest in the work of the Mission, and it was to him that Father Drumgoole had written occasional letters about the Home he loved.

"The place is now a garden spot," ran one letter, "though rude and almost uncultivated when we took possession of it a little less than four years ago. . . . The abundance of the crops of every sort attracts the attention of all the neighbors. . . . Mount Loretto has made such an impression on visitors by its beauty that they have pronounced it one of the most interesting places in the state of New York, if not in all America."

In July of 1887 Father Drumgoole received another approval of his work from Rome, the sixth since 1881. Even at that early day, Pope Leo XIII had said to Archbishop Corrigan, when he made the request for the blessing, "Oh, yes, I know about his work and I willingly bless it and him."

St. Anne's chapel at Mount Loretto had long since proved inadequate for the constantly growing family. The church Father Drumgoole was planning to build would be large and modeled after one in Rome, S. Andrea della Valle, in accordance with a suggestion made by Cardinal Parocchi.

During that year Father Drumgoole also received the Holy Father's authorization for a painting which would show the Pope receiving Archbishop McCloskey at the time he went to Rome to receive his red hat, and this he

planned to place in the new church. The Holy Father had
suggested the inclusion in the painting of the portraits of
certain dignitaries who had been present on that occasion,
and explained exactly the place in the picture that should
be occupied by the Roman and Swiss guards.

Of course it was only natural that the Holy Father
should be deeply interested in Mount Loretto and its new
church. All the members of the Union were deeply interested, and he, too, was a member.

During the year 1887 Father Drumgoole heard that certain criticisms had been leveled against *The Homeless
Child* by the Baltimore Council. Father Drumgoole not
only made a categorical denial but cited the many prelates
who were subscribers at home and in Canada, Germany,
France, and Ireland. And he mentioned its most distinguished member, Pope Leo XIII.

Why anyone, save through envy, should level such a
criticism was not clear. Over the years *The Homeless Child*
had hardly changed its format or its contents. It contained
brief lives of the saints with engravings from good paintings, and these Father Drumgoole included so that his
readers, many of whom he had feared knew nothing about
them, might learn of these great men and women of their
Church. There were the reports he made to the archdiocese, and the poems on St. Joseph or Our Lady, usually written by members of the Union, and sometimes the
sermon of a prelate. In addition he published letters from
converts telling him that it was this little magazine which
had started them on the road to Truth. What could be
criticized about all this?

Another accusation, according to the rumors, was that
he received "private help" for his own needs. Those who
heard this were amused rather than irritated, for it was

clear it came from those who had never known the simplicity of his way of life, his few possessions, the clothing he wore year after year until someone forced him to buy a new suit or cloak. Once he had worn a cloak for more than a year without noticing that it had no sleeves; he had picked up an old one which was to be thrown away and had used it until someone objected.

He felt he must explain and defend himself from these vague accusations, and did so in the next number of *The Homeless Child*. During the early difficult days of the Home, he wrote, he had been helped personally by relatives and friends, but he had never used for his own needs a penny given him for his Mission. Years before, a loyal friend, realizing that Father Drumgoole had certain personal expenses and no income of his own, had put $5,000 in a bank in his name so that he would never need to use the smallest amount of Union funds for himself. But much of that amount still remained in the account; he had used less than half of it.

In his early days he had paid his own way, he explained, and had earned much of it; only the cost of his priesthood training had been met in part by his friends. He had set aside, he said, of the money sent him to the Mission, $200 yearly for Masses for those who helped clothe and educate poor children in their own parishes, and he sent these sums for Mass intentions to missionary priests in distant lands. "In dedicating myself to the Mission," he wrote in *The Homeless Child*, "I gave it my heart and all my worldly goods with it, and since I have no one depending on me since the death of my mother, my worldly goods will belong to the Mission after my death."

As a matter of fact, the Mission property was no longer even in his name nor did he have any personal claim on it.

Long ago he had transferred it to the Mission of the Immaculate Virgin, which was an incorporated institution and under archdiocesan control. "I will leave nothing undone to preserve it intact," he had told the Archbishop at that time, "and so after my death it will continue to save hundreds of thousands of souls."

That very year he had asked an accountant of the archdiocese to go over the Mission accounts. This expert, when he finished, complimented Father Drumgoole. The system used was so clear that one could see at a glance the financial condition of the Mission. This was true also, he said, of the special account carrying the sums set aside for Mass intentions.

This "special account" had grown with the years. Missionary bishops and priests in Asia and India and Africa benefited from it, and over the years more than 50,000 had been aided by Mass stipends and they in turn had given their aid. Money often went through the Archbishop to the bishop of some poor foreign diocese. "One hundred dollars are enclosed, and the intentions are for the most destitute souls in Purgatory," Father Drumgoole would write. Sums went to a church at Nepal, India, to Father O'Keefe in Nassau, in the West Indies, to "an old Roman bishop who has written Your Grace for intentions," to the Franciscan Fathers—and this letter contained the promise of more help, "after March first, when our cow calves." To each contribution was always added the same request —that the Masses be said for the most neglected souls in Purgatory.

In the pages of his little yearly magazine he told the Union members of all these expenditures. He said he knew they would be happy to help since for some of those aided this money had been at times their sole income.

There was no record that any member of the Union had ever objected to this use of the funds.

And each year, in varying words but with the same basic statement, he printed the question that was asked him again and again: "Where does all the money come from that pays for the new houses and the children's care and the many other expenses?" And he answered always, "It comes from the chief source of revenue we have to rely on —the fund created by the twenty-five-cent annual subscription to *The Homeless Child*. From this we have built not only the City House but defrayed all the necessary expenses of the publications of St. Joseph's Union and all the indebtedness incurred in carrying on the work of the Mission of the Immaculate Virgin. For the income from the Mission from every source is always less than the expenditures. This indebtedness which is very large is also paid from the fund created by the annual subscription to *The Homeless Child*."

These reports were always much alike, and they usually ended, "We thank our friends and hope that God will bless them for the donations they have made to the Mission." And he would repeat again his proud statement, "There is no cent of debt against any of our works."

14

->>>

A "Substitute" for Rome

EVERYONE at Mount Loretto took part in the ceremony of
breaking ground for their new church on the feast of Our
Lady's Nativity in 1887. It was a lovely day at summer's
end; the ripples on the bay were gentle. The trees waved
in a little breeze as the long line walked in procession to
the site of the new church—priests, acolytes, religious, employees, and children, all singing as they went.

At the Mass earlier that morning thanksgiving to God
for the favors and blessings bestowed on the Holy Father
had been offered. It was his year of jubilee; for ten years
he had been on the throne of Peter and in his sermon
Father Drumgoole told his large family that the new
church would be dedicated to God in honor of Pope
Leo XIII.

Father Drumgoole, armed with a new and shining spade,
dug the first sod himself, close to the cord which marked
the foundation lines. Then each priest in turn dug a piece
of sod, and one was dug for each of the Sisters who themselves removed from the ground her own bit of turf, as did
all the employees and each of the children who were old
enough. Father Drumgoole blessed the site. After that they
all knelt together under the bright sky and, led by Father
Drumgoole, they prayed that this great undertaking for
God would not fail, that in future years the cross on this

church would be a landmark, a sign to those who came from over the ocean that America belonged to God.

Archbishop Corrigan had already given his promise that he would come to bless the cornerstone which, it was hoped, could be laid early the following year. The work of excavation was to begin soon. As yet, of course, the church was only architects' drawings and a hole in the ground, but already Father Drumgoole visioned it as finished, and was going on to his next project—the building which was to house his cherished trade school. There were many children at Mount Loretto now who would be benefited by such a school, and he was eager to make it a reality. As soon as the church was up he would submit his plans for the next structure.

This did not mean that he was for a moment forgetting the others in his care, for there were many who could not be given such training for some years—little children who must be made strong and healthy and given good training in their faith and a primary education before a trade was even thought of for them. And there were the others, those whom he had the joy of seeing returned to their families after a stay at the Mission. For very often he took small children into his Home in order to give their parents a chance to get on their feet, and then his greatest joy was to send a child back to an unbroken home. Those returned were not given back haphazardly, for parents had to give proof that they would care for them and had to promise to send them to church and to school. And also the Society for the Prevention of Cruelty to Children had to be fully satisfied regarding the conditions that awaited the children who had been under his care.

They worked well together, the Society and Father Drumgoole, who knew that its work had saved many children from degraded parents and from those who wanted to use them for some selfish purpose, children who could be reached in no other way than through the officers of such an organization. Elbridge Gerry, its founder, had come out to Mount Loretto that year and later spoke of it as a "model," a place that not only educated children to be good citizens but taught them "that there is a God to worship and a religion to follow."

Father Drumgoole had told him that he was sorry he could not take even more children from him, but that he now had 1,300 in his homes and, until he could add more space, must limit himself to what he called "hardship cases." He did not like to be so limited, for he wanted to give help to every child that needed it. Above all he wanted such children to be placed where they would have spiritual as well as material care.

"I sincerely trust," Mr. Gerry wrote him a little later, "you will not forget in your prayers the Society for the Prevention of Cruelty to Children, and that the interest you have always so practically shown in your long and laborious work of caring for helpless little ones in this city will continue to find its echo in your appreciation of this Society which stands always ready to second your praiseworthy and most excellent efforts in their behalf."

It was true that there were many unusual features about Mount Loretto, but no doubt the outstanding one was the way in which the spiritual life was interwoven into the daily routine. The children lived very literally close to God. They attended a short daily Mass, marching in long columns through the connecting passages of the main buildings, chattering as they went, for conversation was never rationed until they came into the chapel. In the earlier years Father Drumgoole had always been the celebrant; now he managed to be there at least every other day. After Mass the children went through the grounds to the dining room, past a flower bed where all spring and until late fall bloomed a floral cross and under it, also in flowers, the words, *"In hoc signo."*

During the day the Sisters managed, along with the pre-scribed studies, to tell the children occasional stories of saints. And always before classes they led them in a brief prayer. Evenings, the smaller ones went for a walk under the tall trees, each little child holding the hand of another small one, Sister watching carefully to see that no one strayed off. Even when they were being tucked into bed, they heard Sister murmur a little prayer over them and often, much later, Father Drumgoole went softly through the dormitories blessing the little sleepers.

There were many visitors to this unusual Home, and often men in high places in church and state. One bishop from Italy said he had seen in his lifetime two miracles: one, when he had in his hands the glass which held the dried blood of St. Januarius and saw it liquefy under his very eyes; the other, Mount Loretto.

In July of 1887 Father Glynn, an Augustinian prior, recently arrived from Rome, came to visit the home. He had heard of this amazing Mission at the Vatican and he wanted to see it for himself. Later he declared that there had been no exaggeration in the reports. "Here you use Christian and not merely anti-poverty principles," he said, and that, thought Father Drumgoole's helper, was a very good summing up of his entire aim.

In the same month Archbishop Corrigan, on his annual visitation of Staten Island, came to Mount Loretto to be Father Drumgoole's guest. Great preparations were made for this visit. Father Glynn and Father Drumgoole went in to New York to meet the Archbishop at the foot of White-hall Street and all three boarded the ferry. The pilothouse at the front had been set aside for the party and they had a fine view of the ships and the islands. The sky was blue; the sails swelled in the river breeze. The statue of Liberty gleamed from her height. At St. George a special train, as well as the band from the city, was waiting.

Father Glynn had been very vocal about the Mission and was still lauding it to the Archbishop. "There they work for the poor and don't merely talk about it," he said enthusiastically, as if he were explaining something new to the prelate. When they reached Mount Loretto even Father Drumgoole, the perfectionist, could have asked for no more than awaited them. The grounds were in perfect order. The cottages looked the acme of neatness. As the carriage passed, 1,000 children cheered and waved and the bell in the tower pealed a welcome.

Around a great harp of flowers on the lawn stood the smallest children, the boys in white, the girls in blue, and when the Archbishop reached the top step of the main building he turned to bless them. He smiled into their up-lifted faces, and on his own was a very tender expression.

It was no wonder, said His Grace, that Father Glynn had been amazed at what he saw. Each time he came there he also felt that same amazement. On this visit he went over the entire place—the dormitories and the offices, the chicken yard and cow barn, the artesian wells, the dock with its floating bath at the pier, the fine machinery in the great barn.

On the way back to the city Father Glynn was still voicing his enthusiasm over Mount Loretto. In his many years as a priest he said he had never seen an institution like it. "I think it is truly the greatest and noblest work of charity ever accomplished by the Christian energy and zeal of one man," he said to the Archbishop. It was a revelation, too, he said, of the work the Church was carrying out in the United States, and he was anxious to tell in Rome what he had seen at Mount Loretto.

In October the plans for the new church were ready, and Father Drumgoole sent them to Rome for approval. Each of its three altars was to be the facsimile of an ancient altar in a Roman church, and these were to be selected in the Holy City. Father Drumgoole had written Cardinal Parocchi that he would be satisfied with any changes made in the plans and they could be made without consulting him further. There was only one addition which he was very anxious to have made to the design of the church, and that was a spire. He explained exactly why he wanted it: "I wish to have one, as it will render the church more conspicuous to steamers entering and leaving the New York Harbor."

At the year's end a parcel came from Rome, accompanied by a letter from the Cardinal. He called it a "small present." On opening it Father Drumgoole found it contained an announcement of the blessing of the Holy Father, sent him during the jubilee year. He showed it next day to everyone he saw—priests, laity, Sisters, and he read it in translation to the children. "No earthly gift could equal it in my estimation," he declared. "And now we must hurry more than ever with our new church which will, in a way, be a memorial of this jubilee." When he wrote to thank the Holy Father, he told him that work would soon start on the foundations of the new church and that the Archbishop had made arrangements to lay and bless the cornerstone on July 26 of the next year.

Cardinal Parocchi had written him that the Holy Father

wished very much to see the American priest who was caring for so many homeless children in America. Father Drumgoole found it difficult indeed to reply.

When he did answer he made it very clear that to come to Rome would be his dearest wish. But to absent himself even for a few months from the Mission, especially now that the building of the church would soon start, added to the fact that he was at work on the annual number of *The Homeless Child,* would be like running away from his responsibilities. But he sighed as he wrote, for he was relinquishing something that would have been the greatest joy he had known in his life of many joys.

"It would afford me the highest earthly pleasure," he wrote, "to get one sight of our Holy Father Leo XIII, and to be enabled to thank personally the Cardinal Vicar for his extraordinary kindness to me. Next to His Holiness there is no one on earth I have a greater desire to see than His Eminence."

His letter was received at Rome with regret. Cardinal Parocchi, taking it to the Pope, remembered a letter he had received a few years earlier, at a time when reports to America said the Holy Father was in actual danger. Father Drumgoole had written offering Mount Loretto as a refuge and a home. The smile that he and the Holy Father had exchanged over that had been very tender.

That same winter Father Drumgoole had to settle the affairs of Yolande de Comeau. On entering the community of the Sisters of St. Francis and before she made her vows, she had given Father Drumgoole $100,000 for a home for blind girls. At that time she had asked that one part of the building be set aside to house a group of Sisters of perpetual adoration, who could come from the ranks of the

Sisters themselves—those too old for the usual duties or those in some way unfitted for active work.

This home for the blind Father Drumgoole planned to begin the following spring. The Archbishop highly approved the project. It would be the first effort made in New York by Catholics to care for the blind.

It was always difficult for Father Drumgoole to put down in his report to the Archbishop everything that had happened; each day something new occurred, just as every day new plans came to him which he wanted to carry out. At the end of 1887 he placed emphasis on those boys who were working on the farm at Mount Loretto, and to whom he was now paying regular farm hands' wages. During vacations some took jobs on neighboring farms, and the employers were always very complimentary about their work. He had begun to receive letters from the West offering good acreage at reasonable prices, and, though this was a matter for the future, he had some of the boys saving to buy farms and studying drainage and soils and other necessary agricultural subjects.

To the Union his letter of 1887 was chiefly an expression of gratitude to these generous people who had made all his work successful and helped it grow each year. Especially he thanked those solicitors all over the world who obtained new subscribers for him: "As an act of gratitude we shall have 500 Masses said this year for the spiritual and temporal welfare of the solicitors," he wrote, "and of all who aid us in obtaining subscriptions. It must be consolation to you and to all the members of the Union to know that at present the Mission shelters about 1,400 in both houses, who, principally through your continual, noble, charitable, and truly Christian efforts are enjoying all the benefits of a Catholic home. . . . Through your united efforts many thousands of poor children are preserved from losing their faith and from ignorance, vice, and degradation."

There followed directions regarding papers and certificates and letters, and he ended by praying that God would bless the Union members "for what you are doing for His suffering members," and begging them to remember him in their prayers and Communions.

During the first months of 1888 Father Drumgoole gave some hours each day—when he could spare them—to the preparation of what he called the "substitute" he was sending to Rome in his place. This was an album containing many views of Mount Loretto. It was a really wonderful affair, for it showed for the first time in one place all the activities of that far-spread mission. There were interior and exterior views of every building erected at Mount Loretto—the chapels, the dormitories, the playgrounds for summer, the recreation rooms for winter. There were pictures of the boiler room, the bakery—"where six barrels of flour are used daily," said the caption—the bathhouse, the bay itself, the barn, still reputed to be the largest in the country, big enough for 200 cows and fifty horses, its upper floors fitted up for the more than fifty farmers employed on the farm. There were pictures of the cottages of the other workers, and always Father Drumgoole was careful to have the family assembled on the porch when the picture was taken. The icehouse was photographed, the carpenter house, the slaughterhouse, the pen where 600 pigs were kept, the hennery, and the rabbit warren.

There were photographs of the various classes of children at the school, of the little ones too small for school, of the boys being trained in trades. The latter were shown tailoring, making shoes, baking, working in engine room, boiler rooms, and dairy. And there was one picture which showed smiling farmers of the future. All these photographs were now being carefully arranged so that the Holy Father and Cardinal Parocchi and their friends could "visit every apartment in every house in Mount Loretto at their leisure."

Then Father Drumgoole decided the City House must be included, and again the photographers went to work and made pictures of everything there from the statues of Our Lady and St. Joseph to the cubicles where each boy had his own place. Since it was still winter, the work sometimes lagged, for the weather was often cloudy and picture-taking was difficult.

There was one photograph which everyone said must be included—that of the Founder himself. This he opposed, as he had always opposed the taking of his picture, but eventually he capitulated. He sighed when they brought him this photograph for approval. "It does look like me," he admitted. "It is very natural." But he still looked uneasy, and helpers quickly pasted it in the book so that he could not change his mind.

In sending the album to Rome he said he hoped it would serve as a substitute for his own presence that year, at least until the church was under way or, even better, finished. "I have no one living to take my place," he wrote, "and everything going on at the present time requires my own immediate presence every day. I have not taken a day's complete relaxation in over nineteen years, and I could not come to Rome now without doing more or less injury to the Mission, which, in conscience, I cannot do under any considerations."

The "substitute" completed, he turned to other work. As soon as he received final approval of his plans from Rome he would begin to build his church.

The plans for the blind girls' home were ready and he discussed them with Yolande de Comeau. She told him of one more gift she wanted to present to the Mission before she made her vows. When he and Father McNichol went with her to her home to get this, they found awaiting them a great pile of plate and much jewelry, which she told them was to be sold at auction and the proceeds given to the Mission.

Father McNichol was awed to note with what indifference she looked at it all. Later, on a visit to Buffalo, Father Drumgoole went to see Yolande at the convent and was greatly impressed at the way this girl who, when she lived in the world, had had every wish anticipated, now carried out the menial duties of a postulant.

During that cold winter snowy days made travel difficult. Father Drumgoole kept to his usual routine of spending alternate days at the City House and at Mount Loretto. Perhaps his greatest joy during this latter part of his life was to go in turn to each of his homes.

He would come to Mount Loretto over the footpath from the station at Pleasant Plains, to see how the farmers were preparing the ground for the spring sowing, to pass by the smithy, to see his children helping the farmers— sitting on a plodding, patient horse or feeding the stock— to walk to the rooms where his boys were learning a trade.

He always gave a look of satisfaction at one small cottage, where Mr. Kernan, formerly an Episcopalian clergyman, taught Latin to those among the older boys who showed a predilection for learning. He hoped that from this group there would come vocations someday, and when he passed the cottage he always said a little prayer for that intention.

All this was good to see, as it was good to pass the place

where the earth had been dug for the new church and where before long the Archbishop would bless the first stone of the edifice which was to house Our Lord and honor the two who were not only His parents but the parents of every child who slept the sleep of carefree childhood in this Mission. He loved the moments when the smaller ones saw him coming and ran to meet him, snuggling under the black cloak that was too small to hold them all yet seemed to expand as they crept under it. And if they grew obstreperous, a few words from him would quiet them and they would trot off to their play again.

He looked after them with his protecting smile. He had always been a quiet man who rarely raised his voice, who never expressed resentment when people hurt him. But if someone hurt his children or spoke ill of them, he roused like a lion, standing always between them and injustice, no matter whether he had to defy parent, charity aid, or legislature.

After a quiet night at Mount Loretto, he would say Mass and go back to the City House for a day and a night there. And that was a joy, too, to look at the great structure that St. Joseph and he had raised, the cross standing at its peak, high over the tired noisy city, to bow to St. Joseph at the southern wall and to lift his hat to Our Lady, her arms outstretched over the entrance. He thought when he first saw the statue in place that she seemed to be saying, "Come to me, little wanderers of the streets," and she had never ceased to say it. And when he entered the house there were the voices of his boys calling, "Hello, Father John," and often in the morning there were the poor being given a meal in St. Joseph's hospitable room.

Next day he was on the road again on the trip by ferry and train to his other Home, saying his rosary on the upper deck, greeted by half the passengers, for he was now so well known that he had become almost a legend. Everyone who passed had a smile for the elderly priest with his crown of snow-white hair—he looked exactly like Pius IX, said those who had seen that Pope—and more than one said they loved to greet him so that they might hear the clear, musical voice in which he answered them.

15

The Great Blizzard—Father Drumgoole's Death

THE WEATHER in early 1888 continued unpleasantly cold and rough, with gales and sleety snow. Both at Staten Island and in the City House his helpers begged Father Drumgoole to make fewer trips back and forth until the weather improved, but he merely laughed at such advice and serenely went his accustomed way.

Those who worked with him had noticed more than once during the past year that Father Drumgoole was losing his accustomed vigor, that his step was slower. But he always waved aside the suggestion that he have a doctor check his condition, just as he had done on his first encounter with illness many years before. But to himself he admitted that sometimes during the day he found himself overcome with a weariness such as he had never known in his strong and active life. His back ached and his head felt heavy, and, worst of all, the symptoms did not disappear even though he applied himself with extra energy to the work before him. One evening he said to Father McNichol, as they sat together for a quiet moment in his little room, "I'm getting old and I'm afraid I may soon be useless."

Father McNichol laughed at his fears, but it was true that his old chief was far from his robust self. His eyes were growing dim; his once-straight shoulders were bent; sometimes one noted a trembling of the hands. "You could take a short rest," he hazarded. "Perhaps that is all you need."

Father Drumgoole looked quizzically at the worried face of his assistant. "I'll tell you my plans. When I'm sure I've got the Mission going without me, I'm going to retire to some quiet monastery. But first the church must be built and the vocational training house. Then I'll go to my old-age retreat."

On March 10 he said Mass as usual at the City House before his return to Mount Loretto. After Mass, Father McNichol, coming into the chapel, saw him kneeling in prayer before Our Lady's altar. His white hair was shining in the light from the window; his arms were outstretched as he so often held them when he was praying, and Father McNichol thought that so must Moses have looked when he was begging God to help his people. Father Drumgoole was praying half-aloud, and something in his attitude made the younger priest think of their earlier conversation. He found himself adding a prayer to Father John's thanksgiving: "Keep him for us, Lord. Watch over him," he prayed.

On the afternoon of Sunday, March 11, a light rain fell, which gradually turned to snow. By night a violent gale had arisen, and at Mount Loretto the Sisters and the resident priests begged Father Drumgoole to forego his usual trip to the city next day. He laughed at their fears and boarded the train at Pleasant Plains as usual. He found it unusually empty for a Monday morning, and when the conductor came through he smiled to see this passenger in his accustomed place.

"Well, you are braver than some of them, Father," he said. "Lots of folks think this will turn into a real blizzard and they're staying home."

Father Drumgoole looked out at the driving snow and for the first time he felt apprehensive. "Think we'll get through all right?"

"Oh, we'll get through all right," said the conductor reassuringly, "but if we'll get back I'm not so sure."

At St. George he found things strangely quiet. And now Father Drumgoole learned that he could go no farther that day. The *Southfield* was making its last trip back until the storm was over, and no other ferries would be allowed to start out to New York. The boat reached the pier, but with difficulty, the flagpoles fore and aft broken off by the fierce wind and its shivering, frightened passengers huddled on the deck. Even Father Drumgoole saw that it was useless to try to get to New York. He decided to take the train back to Pleasant Plains. But at the gate the official shook his head. "No more trains till further notice," he said.

Father Drumgoole pondered what to do. He could stay in St. George, of course, but it would be better to get to Mount Loretto while there was still an opportunity. He hired a horse and gig from a man he knew and set out for home.

How he made it perhaps he himself hardly knew, but in the early afternoon a Sister, looking from the window at the stormy world before her, saw a horse and gig coming slowly up the drive. She called to the others and they brought the exhausted man into the house, while one of the hastily summoned workers took the tired horse to the barn.

It was not until some days later that communication was restored to Mount Loretto, which had been entirely isolated. There was no getting about at all, save with difficulty, from house to house and house to barn. But the fires had not failed and the children had been fed. Because the storm had occurred on a Sunday, many of the cooks and bakers who had gone to New York for the week end had not been able to return to work. The Sisters had baked the many loaves needed for the hundreds of children and cooked the meals, and had done their best to keep their charges warm and happy and unafraid.

By Tuesday the storm abated, but on Wednesday the wind's velocity was still eighty-five miles an hour. Not until Thursday did any trains begin to run to Pleasant Plains. The drifts were so high in many places that tunnels were dug from house to road. Trees had been uprooted and dead birds lay everywhere. Most people had not left their homes at all, but some who did had been exhausted by their struggle to get through the drifted snow and now their deaths were reported.

At Mount Loretto, when the full danger of Father Drumgoole's trip from St. George was fully realized, many prayers of thanksgiving were sent up for his safe homecoming. He himself seemed no worse for the ordeal, though he had developed a cough which worried the Sisters. He merely laughed at their anxiety: when one considered the real tragedies of the storm, surely a cough was nothing to give thought to. Nevertheless they won from him a promise that he would stay at Mount Loretto until the weather gave definite promise of betterment. Word had come from New York of the ravages of the storm there—of streets piled high with snow, of broken telephone poles coated with a foot of ice. No one had ventured from the City House on the day of the storm, and on Thursday Father Drumgoole learned to his relief that no one there had been hurt, no one had suffered. The City House had resumed its usual tasks and they all hoped, the message ran, that

Father Drumgoole would rest at Mount Loretto until travel was completely restored.

On St. Joseph's feast day Father Drumgoole said Mass in St. Anne's chapel. He gave a short sermon to the children on the Patron of the Universal Church who was also their special patron. He spoke of his love for the Child entrusted to him and through Him of his love for every child. Always, he said, they were to remember that St. Joseph would help them in their difficulties now and in the future; always they were to call with confidence on him. When they grew older and left Mount Loretto, when difficulties came into their lives, and when earthly help seemed failing them, they were to remember that St. Joseph would not fail them.

"Now you trust me to take care of you," he said. "But when I am not with you to counsel you or anyone to turn to, never, my dear children, never yield to despair. Turn to St. Joseph. He has never failed me, not once in my life. He will not fail you either."

After Mass he made his first trip to the city after the storm. Train service was quite restored, though snow still lay deep on the surrounding fields. The ferries were running normally and many people greeted him when they saw his familiar black cloak back on the upper deck.

In New York he was welcomed back with joy by his household, and he promised that since he had been so long away he would stay a few days with them before he returned to Mount Loretto. He seemed well, they all thought, though a little tired, and the Sisters gave him a syrup to help the insistent cough.

On Palm Sunday he said Mass as usual and preached a short sermon, but he did not look well. The ruddy glow on his cheeks was missing and he looked haggard. But his smile was as kind, his words as vigorous, and his attentions to his boys as thoughtful as ever. So those about him stopped worrying, for he went about his work as usual. Only the annoying cough remained, and the Sisters doctored that faithfully.

On Monday morning, as he was preparing to rise at four o'clock to say his Mass, he suddenly felt his strength go from him. He fell to the floor and found he was too weak to rise. He called for help but not until he managed to rap on the wall could he attract attention to his plight. Two boys passing the door heard the rapping and his weak call for help.

He was lifted back into his bed and a doctor hastily summoned. It did not take him long to make the diagnosis. Father Drumgoole had pneumonia, no doubt from a cold caught on the day of the fearful snowstorm, for the doctor said he had evidently been suffering from it for some time. He should have been called in earlier, he said reproachfully, to have been of any help.

When the Sisters gathered about the doctor as he came from the sickroom and asked in deep anxiety how serious was his condition, the doctor said bluntly, "He is only a shell. He is worked out."

Father Drumgoole lay quietly in his bed, his big black rosary wound round his wrist. He smiled when the doctor and the Sister who was to care for him came to tell him that his condition was serious. In fact, the doctor told him bluntly that he was close to death because treatment had been too long delayed; both lungs were seriously affected.

His face was serene even after he heard this verdict and he smiled reassuringly into the faces of the two bending over him. Then he grew sober. "God's will be done," he said, but he added in a wistful tone, "I had hoped to live a little longer to advance the work of the Mission. But God's will be done," he repeated, and this time he spoke very firmly.

He asked Father McNichol to say his Mass for the members of the Union that morning. Long ago, at the very inception of that organization, he had promised to say Masses daily for them—"as long as I can stand up." This was his first failure—and not really a failure, for his heart was at the altar with Father McNichol.

During the morning he made his confession and received Viaticum. When the Blessed Sacrament was brought into the room, those about him noticed he was making an effort of some kind. They soon realized he was trying to rise and kneel before his Lord. He was gently restrained and told he had not the strength, that Our Lord would understand his intention.

After he had been anointed, he asked the Sister with him for the picture of Pope Leo XIII, which was one of his greatest treasures. On it were written the words of the Pope's blessing for Father John Christopher Drumgoole in the hour of his death and granting him the plenary indulgence. He looked long at the face of the Pontiff, smiled and nodded, as if bowing his thanks for the favor granted him, and told them to put the picture back in its place on the table.

His mind still alert, he turned to the matter of his temporal interests, since he had now completed the spiritual, and at intervals that Tuesday morning he arranged with his assistants the affairs of the Mission. When this was done, and the plans for the new church had been scrutinized once more, he said, "All I possess is my poor children's. Everything belongs to them. For them I have worked and fought. It is their cause I shall take with me and continue pleading."

He made a will, leaving everything he had, real and personal, to the Mission. He was able to sign only with difficulty, and Father McNichol, thinking of the firm, running signature to which he was accustomed, was moved at the sight of this shakily written name, legible only to one who knew what it was meant to be.

Last of all, Father Drumgoole arranged that a sum be sent to a little convent of nuns in Africa, so that they would be able to have Masses said—"for the poor souls in Purgatory." It was for the poor souls that, since the day of his ordination, he had offered all his work; it was for their intention that he asked for Masses with every stipend he sent throughout the world.

He then asked Father McNichol to bring him a paper from his desk—a letter from Lord Rosebery. The younger priest found letters wrapped around the picture of a handsome young man in a silver frame. "I have never left your house," ran one brief note, "without feeling better for it and without feeling that I had got an insight into a higher and holier life than men are generally privileged to lead or indeed are capable of leading. God bless you—if that may be said to you without presumption. Rosebery."

Father McNichol looked at the quiet figure on the bed and thought that the letter was an exact expression of his own feelings. He found another letter and knew this was the one which Father Drumgoole wanted. It was very brief: "Do not forget me in your prayers," and bore the same signature. He brought this to the sick man, who smiled as he held the lines closer to his eyes so that he could read them. "I never failed him. Now you must carry on in my place," he said.

That afternoon Archbishop Corrigan came hurrying down to Lafayette Street, having learned of the seriousness of his old friend's illness. He sat by Father Drumgoole's bed and talked with him, gently and comfortingly. Looking about the room, as bare now as it had been when he lived in the small room on Warren Street, his eyes lighted on the picture of St. Joseph at the head of the bed. "I see you have St. Joseph very near you," he said.

The sick man nodded earnestly. "Oh, I couldn't live without him," he said, and then, in a low and very tired voice, he added, "nor die without him."

After the Archbishop blessed him and said good-by, Father Drumgoole went back to his prayers, his old black beads tight in his hand. It grew dark, and after a long time dawn came, and those beside him knew he had never stopped praying. His only interruption was when the watchers at his bedside urged him to rest a while, to try to get some sleep.

The day wore on, and during much of it Father Drumgoole's mind wandered. Now and then he raised his hand as if blessing the children, and sometimes he called one by name. Sometimes he seemed to be preaching, for he spoke about Our Lady. Once, at a time when his mind was clear, he said to Father McNichol, "The children—please have all the children at my requiem Mass." And once he said very clearly, "I won't get to Rome next year, after all."

Now and then he murmured a few words which were interpreted by the watchers as aspirations though they could distinguish no words. Toward evening they heard him say in a clear voice, "Jesus, Mary, Joseph, I love you," and every word was distinctly spoken. After that his breathing grew difficult and then very faint.

Round about him the priests and the Sisters recited the

prayers for the dying, and as they neared the end it was seen that he had ceased to breathe. The bells of the Angelus rang the end of day, and to those listening by the bedside it was like a gentle knell for the dying of a gentle man.

Everyone was weeping, his priests for the loss of a friend, his Sisters for the loss of a father. In the chapel of the City House his orphans were praying for him and most of them were crying. A world—even a house—without Father John in it simply could not be imagined. When they had heard the whispered words, "Father John is dead," they had broken into tears, unashamed, as children do when someone who has taken care of them is gone. The older people knew there would be others to take up the work, but the young felt only the immediate loss, the terror of being alone. And especially strong was the feeling of these children rescued by him from the streets, from neglect, even from cruel treatment.

The hundreds who came to the door a little later, to get their soup and bread in St. Joseph's room, also wept when they heard that Father John was gone. And these were not children, but men and women whose hearts were often long closed to feeling. But the man who had fed them and had often come to speak to them comfortingly would speak words of comfort no more, and they wept his loss.

On his death certificate the first cause of death was stated as exhaustion, the secondary was pneumonia. As one of his friends well phrased it, in feeding the lamp of charity he had exhausted the lamp of life.

When the news reached an anxious Mount Loretto and the children learned that their Father John was dead, they would not believe it. Father John was different. Other people died—parents and brothers and sisters—but not Father

John. He was necessary to one's day; he came to bless them when the night was dark; he played with them in recreation room and playground. At intervals next day, when wheels were heard on the drive or voices on the porch, the very little children rushed out to meet him as usual, and their faces wore a bewildered look when Father John did not come.

Holy Thursday came and Good Friday, doubly sad this year to his family and his friends. His body, vested as for Mass, was taken from his room to the largest room at the Home. At each side of the coffin stood boys of the Mission, in white shirts and black trousers and ties. A Sister stood at the head of the coffin and from time to time children and Sisters were replaced in the guard of honor.

The streets outside were filled with people who had come to take their places in the ranks of those who wanted to see for the last time the man who had been good to them or of whose goodness they had heard from those he had helped. As the people passed along there was complete silence, broken only by the shuffling of feet and the occasional clicking of a rosary as it was lifted to touch the hands that lay over Father John's breast where his own rosary was twined as it had always been. Many in the long lines knelt and asked his intercession, for there was a general belief that he was already with God. In the great crowds—it was estimated that at least 100,000 passed the coffin during the days he lay there—were children he had befriended, poor he had fed, rich and important people, lowly and poor, young and old, some hobbling on crutches, some infirm with age. It was with difficulty that his vestments, even the lining of his coffin, were protected from those who wanted to bear away some relic that had touched him.

"Grief dulls our pen," wrote the editor of the *Catholic Review* a few days later. For it had been so unexpected. People had seen him only the week before, full of life and hope, and planning for the church which was to be built in honor of the Holy Father. That week he had spoken of an additional plan—to build on the grounds at Mount Loretto a reproduction of the little House of Loretto. And he had been talking of the plans for his next big building —the trade school. It seemed incredible that this man who dealt in futures would not carry out these plans.

Not only the Catholic press wrote his eulogy. The *Herald,* which could be very caustic in political matters, had only words of affection here: "His name was a household word in every city and town throughout this broad land, as well as in foreign countries. And wherever the *Herald* was read yesterday the same grief came to those familiar with his work. Few men have lived in this age whose deaths have commanded such widespread and heartfelt regrets."

Then the reporter spoke of the results of his work among destitute city children: "He went into the highways and byways, to the water front, wherever he thought to find a little vagrant. . . . Today there are hundreds of young men prospering in different walks of life here and elsewhere who can attribute all they now possess of success and respectability to the patient, earnest exhortations and saving help of Father Drumgoole."

In the *Freeman's Journal* the editor, Maurice Francis Egan, wrote a long editorial on him: "No merely human power could have done what Father Drumgoole did; genius could not have done it; wealth could not have done it; both combined might have done much; but only supreme and impregnable faith could have done what he has done. . . .

Credulous but shrewd, easily imposed on but prudent; strong yet gentle; homely in manners, yet the truest gentleman at heart. . . . He changed the vicious child of the street into a self-respecting and neighbor-respecting Christian. He was a national benefactor. May he rest in peace!"

But it was a friend of Father Drumgoole who perhaps best expressed it when he said the epitaph for him might well be the words of Goldsmith on his own father:

> His house was known to all the vagrant train;
> He chid their wanderings but relieved their pain.

And it was Monsignor Preston who said what many felt: "I think that I can safely say that we may pray to him instead of for him."

On Easter Sunday, after his body was brought to St. Patrick's Cathedral, crowds again came to pass by his bier. That evening the Office of the Dead was chanted.

On Easter Monday, in a cathedral where one seemed still to hear the echoes of the joyous feast of the day before, his funeral was held. The great church was filled with hundreds of bishops and priests and lay people come to pay their last respects. The pallbearers were the trustees of the Mission of the Immaculate Virgin, and a guard of honor of twelve senior boys from the Home stood about the catafalque. In pews near by were Sisters of St. Francis and Sisters of Charity. The coffin was open. Father John lay in his purple chasuble. The rugged face was very much as he had looked in life.

The celebrant of the Mass was Archbishop Corrigan, with Monsignor Farley assisting him. Father Landry, come from Niagara University to do a last service for his old student and friend, was deacon of honor. In the sanctuary were the two boys who were the first fruits of his search for vocations—John McCormick and Charles Cassidy, both to be ordained the following year.

Monsignor Preston read a cablegram from Rome, expressing the Holy Father's sorrow at the death of the priest whom he had so much wanted to see in person. The grand choir sang Cherubini's Mass of Requiem and then Archbishop Corrigan performed the ceremony of absolution and the coffin was closed.

When it was all over, the body was taken to Mount Loretto. A long line of funeral coaches followed the hearse down Fifth Avenue and Broadway to the ferry. At St. George a special train was waiting.

The house at Staten Island had been wrapped in deep sorrow since the word had come of Father Drumgoole's death. The weather since the great storm had been gray and the air was damp and chill even inside the house. There were great patches of snow, witnesses of the blizzard of a few weeks before. Spring was on the way but winter still ruled.

There was unusual silence throughout house and grounds, none of the customary noise of shouting and laughter. The older children who really understood what had happened went about their duties with faces on which were often seen unashamed tears. The smaller ones, though aware that something had happened to their Father John, were still only half-comprehending.

Of the older children some were not unaccustomed to sadness. Many had known the loss of parents, had come from the darkness of New York's tenements to the beauty and pastoral charm of Mount Loretto, to live good days there, playing and singing and studying and working and learning the faith that permeated a home where Father John was everywhere.

They were all too young to realize the real nobility of one who had taken them in to care for them when others could not or would not. But they all could know and feel the father's affection he had given them, as he walked among them as though he were merely a workman in the great structure he had himself built. He had time for them, time to listen to their stories, to play their games, and even to tease them. Not one boy or girl there but had felt Father John's hand patting his head; none had ever been made to feel unwanted or had gone unnoticed by him. He was the father of each one of them.

To the little children his death was confusing. He had gone to God, to heaven, they were told. During those next days they talked about him a great deal. Gradually the deep sadness went away, for childish grief is a resilient thing, but they continued to talk about him. Where would he be in heaven, they wondered.

"With the saints, of course," said one. "He's a saint, my mother told me, and that's where he belongs."

"Then he must have a name the way saints do," said another.

What was he to be called? What name would Our Lord give him? The favorite name chosen was St. John of Mount Loretto, but when one lad presented St. Father John, this was conceded the best title of all.

On the day he came home for his burial the sun broke through the overcast heavens. The sky became blue with white clouds drifting across it as the funeral cortege came slowly to Mount Loretto.

In the chapel Father Landry sang the Mass. Father Mc-Nichol gave a brief sermon. He spoke of John Christopher Drumgoole's fine life, of his good death, of how the Holy Father had wanted to see this priest of whom he had heard such fine things from visitors to the Mission. He told of the honors offered Father Drumgoole, and how he had gently refused every honor, saying he did not want them. "What you have to give, give to my children," he had asked, and the response had been generous, an answer of love to a man who asked only for gifts of love given in love.

He was buried on the sloping woodland in the little cemetery where children who had died at the Home were buried. Many of those who had been at the rites at the Cathedral were not present. But his family was there, hundreds of the little boys and big boys, the little girls and older girls, and when he was taken from the chapel to the burying ground they formed a procession that stretched all the way from the door of the chapel to his grave. In the procession was every one of his children and every grownup who worked at Mount Loretto and every Sister who had helped him there in his work of love.

Afterward the procession of children walked slowly back from the cemetery. Usually they would have broken ranks after a procession, but this time they stayed in close lines all the way back to their home.

16

‣➤➤➤➤➤➤➤➤➤➤➤➤➤➤➤➤➤➤➤➤➤➤➤➤➤➤➤➤➤

Epilogue

AMONG THOSE who knew Father Drumgoole there was considerable apprehension regarding the ability of any other man to carry on a work so peculiarly his, a work which, despite its immense growth with the years, he had managed practically alone. Under the direction of another it might, they feared, fall into difficulties. The Archbishop himself, troubled about this, had, some months before Father Drumgoole's death, held a long discussion with him regarding the latter's idea of establishing a religious congregation to take over his work, a group patterned after the Salesian congregation of Don Bosco, whose methods he greatly admired.

"I have three excellent priests assisting me now," he said, "but not one has a special calling to devote himself to this work and all will someday no doubt be called by Your Grace to other work outside the Mission. Any man who takes over a work like this, even if he has deep piety and zeal and learning, will not succeed unless he has also love of children and sympathy with them."

The two need not have worried, for the man chosen by the Archbishop as Father Drumgoole's successor was well fitted to become the new head of the Mission. Nevertheless, Father Dougherty, pastor of St. Monica's Church in

215

New York City, was overcome when the Archbishop sent for him and told him of the task he wished him to undertake, and said he did not believe he could ever carry it out. And when he realized that he must accept, he knelt to beg of the Archbishop his blessing—and his prayers.

During the next years many of Father Drumgoole's cherished plans were to come to fruition under the sympathetic and understanding leadership of the new director. The building of the church, though delayed, went forward. The employment office was formally opened and soon had to be enlarged. It was learned from the files that during the last year of Father Drumgoole's life he had placed 498 boys in good positions; it was evident that such a work filled a great need and Father Dougherty continued to add to that fine record.

The asylum for the blind was built, the gift of Yolande de Comeau, now Sister Mary Ann of the Franciscan community; in 1900 she herself came again to Staten Island as superior of the house. She established an industrial room for the girls, fitted with looms, and she was still at work on new ideas for her beloved blind when she died in 1918, after nearly twenty years of happy work among them.

The trade school building was completed in 1889, a sturdy five-story building. When, some months later, it was blessed by Monsignor Farley, there was a big procession, and in it the proudest of all were Father Dougherty in his cassock and the trades' apprentices in their clean blue overalls. The machines were in place for sawing and planing, for cloth and fabric work. There was a fine library, a good reading room, and over these a dormitory with baths. Father Drumgoole would have rejoiced to see his dream become fact in brick and stone.

In September 1891 the cornerstone of the new Church of St. Joachim and St. Anne was laid. And when several years later the building was ready, a photograph of it was sent to Pope Leo XIII, who had in fact himself chosen its design and in whose honor—because Father Drumgoole knew how great a devotion the Holy Father had for St. Joachim—the church was named. Word came from the Cardinal Vicar that the Holy Father was delighted with the gift and had had it hung in a room in his private apartments.

The church was indeed a beautiful structure. Its spire rose 225 feet above the ground and, as Father Drumgoole had planned, it was so tall that its cross would be one of the last things seen by ships leaving the harbor, one of the first to greet the eyes of passengers on incoming ships. The high altar was the gift of the De Comeau family, his great friends. Its interior was Gothic and its upper walls were pierced by small stained-glass windows. Below these were great stained-glass windows, the work of Munich artists. Each illustrated a scene from the New Testament, and all those depicted in them belonged to Biblical times—save in the case of one.

This one exception illustrated the text, "Suffer little children to come to me," and showed Our Lord seated, and all about him children and mothers with children in their arms. On the right of the picture stood Father Drumgoole, directing several small children to Our Lord. He was gesturing with his right hand, calling Him to the attention of two little boys in the skirts and jackets that the smallest children wore when first he founded his Home. Back of them St. Joseph and Our Lady watched him and his children.

Ever since Father Dougherty had undertaken his task at Mount Loretto he had known the need of more Sisters than the Congregation at Buffalo felt it could spare him. When the asylum for the blind, planned by Father Drumgoole, was opened, Father Dougherty knew that the less than fifty Sisters at Mount Loretto and the City House could no longer carry the burden. His request for more Sisters from the motherhouse at Buffalo met with another refusal.

Meantime a new Rule passed by the Buffalo Congregation was found to contain so many points impossible to carry out at Mount Loretto that eventually, in July of 1893, the New York Sisters became a separate community with the title of Sisters of St. Francis of the Mission of the Immaculate Virgin, conventuals of the Third Order. The fact that their title included the name of the Home itself showed how closely their entire congregation was vowed to the work to which Father Drumgoole had called them.

The first mother general of the new community, who had been for some years superior at Mount Loretto, was Mother Mary Catherine. She was the Mary Wallace who had many years ago entered the religious life through the encouragement of Father Drumgoole when he was a seminarian at Our Lady of Angels Seminary and she a young woman who cared for the altars of the little Canadian church where he served as summer helper.

In May of 1898 took place the solemn consecration of the Church of St. Joachim and St. Anne, with Bishop Farley as celebrant of the Mass and Archbishop Corrigan presiding. One incident which occurred that day would have greatly delighted the heart of the Founder. As the day marked the silver jubilee of the Archbishop, the Mission gave recognition to this event in a charming way. At the dinner in his honor following the Mass, a small girl from the Mission recited before him a poem in his honor. She did it very quietly and clearly, with no affectation or fear. But when she came to the end she looked around as if bewildered and then, her eye lighting on Father Dougherty, she ran to him and threw herself into his arms. It was an entirely unrehearsed part of the program and it made one visitor say, "Surely that is no homeless or friendless child." Moreover, such an artless gesture should have reassured any who might have feared that Father Dougherty could not take the place of the Founder. Evidently here was the sort of priest whom Father Drumgoole himself would have chosen, one to whom he could entrust his children.

The speaker who represented St. Vincent's Conferences on this occasion was a happy choice, too. This was James Dougherty, Father Drumgoole's friend and helper of many years, from the time he had helped him with his boys' clubs until the last days when he witnessed his will and followed his coffin to the Cathedral and to the cemetery at Mount Loretto. His heart was full and he found it hard to speak, but he managed to convey to His Grace the hearty good wishes of all the St. Vincent de Paul Conferences on his jubilee.

The two represented well the man who was gone—the little child set in the midst of the priests, the layman who represented the work of St. Vincent after whom Father Drumgoole had patterned his work.

In 1900 was completed the mortuary chapel where Father Drumgoole's remains were to rest permanently and it was consecrated by Bishop Farley, with the Archbishop present. The day chosen was Thanksgiving Day, an appropriate occasion, for it was the reunion day for the old boys and also a day which Father Drumgoole had always used as a time to speak of patriotism and unselfishness to his children.

This chapel was built on an elevation overlooking the buildings of Mount Loretto. On its altar stood a marble statue of the Immaculate Conception. Two circular windows of soft blue glass cast shadows of a softer blue on the stone over his grave. For twelve years he had lain in his grave in the earth; now he was transferred to this lovely replica of the House of Loretto, dedicated to Our Lady under the title he loved.

After Mass had been said, they left him again with his Sisters and his children and the De Comeau family and the few soldiers who had been children here and had been brought home for burial. He lay at the feet of Our Lady. One of the windows represented Christ with His mother, the other Christ with St. Joseph. The Holy Family had been with him all his life; in death they were still around him.

To Mount Loretto and to the City House World War I came and took toll of its boys. During those years the houses were often thronged with khaki-clad soldiers come to say good-by to their alma mater and their friends. When they returned on leave, they told with delight how the military drill taught them at the Home had made their new task much easier and that more than one officer had asked where they, who had not been soldiers before, had received such fine training. And they were proud to answer, "At Mount Loretto."

At the City House, too, the younger boys gave evidence of their patriotism by buying war bonds with their savings. In all, the two houses of the Mission bought more than

$10,000 worth of these. And gold stars marked the loss of many, bringing sorrow to those who considered these boys as their own children.

In other ways the Mission continued as in Father Drumgoole's day. During the winters in the City House thousands of the poor were given breakfast. At Christmas they were given dinners, and, no matter how large the number, Father Drumgoole's rule, that no one be turned away, was still observed. Yearly more than a hundred of the Mission children were reunited with parents or other relatives. In the early years Father Drumgoole had established a department for girls chiefly because he wanted brothers and sisters to live near one another. The latest statistics at Mount Loretto show that there are more than 150 families represented there now, with totals of three to six children in each family.

The sending of mission intentions continued, too. It had amazed those who took over the work after his death to learn how far their Founder was known and how wide had been his charity to missionary priests. From little churches in Ireland came letters of sorrow about his death; from small missions in distant Africa and India they came, and one from one tiny mountain church in the far north of France.

Unfailing also was the response of the Sisters whom Father Drumgoole had long ago begged from the Bishop of Buffalo. Each year more Sisters came to care for the growing number of boys, and later of the girls.

Perhaps representative of all these religious was Sister Angelica who in 1944 was to celebrate her diamond jubilee. Long ago—more than fifty years before that date—she had come to work at the Mission on Lafayette Street, and in all those years she had never failed the boys who lived there. Many people said she was more like the Founder than anyone. She was the one who remembered everyone's feast day, who mothered all the children, and would never admit that any child was bad. One Christmas, when a Sister thought it a good idea to utilize the occasion to stress that Santa Clause would bring gifts only to children who were good, Sister Angelica made it privately clear to them that they were all good and all deserved gifts. She was like Father Drumgoole in that she could never bear to see a child disappointed, and, like him, she strove to keep unhappiness from children.

Her favorite topic was always her boys. "They're just as hungry as they ever were," she would say, her brown eyes twinkling. "They always liked to help me around the kitchen and dining room because then they are nearer the ice box."

At the time of her diamond jubilee the City House was only a memory, but Sister Angelica, looking over the broad acres of Mount Loretto, still spoke with affection of the "big ten story building" where she had spent so many busy useful years.

St. Joseph's Union, which was responsible for all these works—the church, the schools, the wherewithal that fed and clothed the children, the very land on which stood all the houses of the Mission—St. Joseph's Union flourished. The thousands and thousands of members the world over no longer saw the spirited, running signature at the close of the letters of appeal, but were all well aware that Father Drumgoole was still asking them to help his children, his destitute, his poor, his beloved. And the response grew with the years.

In 1894 a statue had been unveiled before the City House, a heroic bronze designed by Robert Cushing. It depicted the well-known tale of Pat, the child whom Lord Rosebery had brought to Father Drumgoole for help and whom the former had helped to rear. The central figure was Father Drumgoole, his breviary and rosary in one hand. The boys on either side of him represented Pat at different stages, one as a ragged newsboy who had wearily thrown down his unsold papers and was reaching for the priest's outstretched hand, the other a neatly dressed boy sitting studying from an open book on his knees.

The unveiling of the statue was a civic occasion, and more than 5,000 people, the *Herald* estimated, attended it. Among the speakers was Elbridge Gerry, head of the Society for the Prevention of Cruelty to Children, Father Drumgoole's lifelong helper and friend. He spoke of the one thing which had most impressed him in his work with Father Drumgoole: "He stood up bravely in practice for the principle of religious instruction accompanying secular studies and he was wise in so doing. The prisons of the state are filled with men who had an education without religion; they are the most dangerous class. The duty of the public is not finished when they clothe a man and fill his stomach." And he ended, "I doubt if any man had the tears of so many children and adults when he died. I doubt if for any individual more prayers are said. As long as the children of the poor have to be rescued and cared for, so long as the city of New York lasts, the memory of Father Drumgoole will live on the earth as certainly as he is immortal in heaven."

At the ceremony the Mission band of seventy-five members furnished the music. There was no doubt but that

Father Drumgoole would have voted it "better than Gilmore's," and that he would have listened with delight when the boys' chorus of 250, standing on the steps and balcony of the Mission house, sang his favorite hymns.

When the speeches and the music were over, the Archbishop drew the veil from the statue. All present were moved at the sight of the familiar figure in cassock and biretta, rosary and breviary in hand, with a child on each side of him.

Twenty-six years later the statue was brought to Mount Loretto to stand in the center of the lawn facing the church Father Drumgoole had planned. Ten feet in height and resting on three huge marble blocks, it was no small undertaking to move it there. The day after it was taken away from the City House, the doorbell there rang and a gentleman who was recognized as Judge Vernon Davies, of the New York Supreme Court and a well-known Episcopal layman, asked what had happened to the statue. When he learned that it was being placed on Staten Island he said sadly, "I am very, very sorry it is gone. Every day when I passed here I raised my hat to that fine man. Something has gone from my life and I shall miss it."

In 1926 the Mission bought the lighthouse and the property around it belonging to the federal government. Built on a knoll seventy feet above sea level, the revolving light in the lighthouse tower for nearly a hundred years had guided the ships that passed on Prince's and Raritan bays. When a newer system of navigation made the light unnecessary, it was put on sale and bought by the Mission. It was then that from the City House was brought the statue of Our Lady that Father Drumgoole had placed there some fifty years before, and which now took its place atop the lighthouse tower—a fitting place for the statue of one whose title is Star of the Sea. It was illuminated for the first time on her own great feast day—that of the Immaculate Conception.

In June 1938 was celebrated the fiftieth anniversary of the death of Father Drumgoole. Cardinal Hayes presided at the Mass which opened the day. There was a colorful procession into the church—acolytes in red and white, schoolboys in blue coats and white flannels, girls in wide straw hats and pretty summer dresses, priests in black and white, monsignori and bishops in purple. In the pews were many of those who had been children in Father Drumgoole's day and many others whose lives were still influenced by his gentle rule.

Monsignor Lavelle preached a sermon on sympathy transformed into practical love and pointed to the results of such a life visible everywhere about them at Mount Loretto. Then—unexpectedly and to the surprise of all—Cardinal Hayes rose to speak.

"I knew him," he said. "Fifty years ago—and just before he died—I paid my first visit to Mount Loretto. I had a long talk with him and was greatly impressed. I see him today as plainly as if he were standing before me. He took me into his room. In one chair, and there were very few, was a statue of St. Joseph. Each morning, so he told me, he took the mail to St. Joseph, considering himself his secretary. That day a letter had called Father Drumgoole a fool. 'Well,' he said to St. Joseph, 'if I am a fool you are a bigger one. For I'm doing your work and you should not let anyone talk to you like that.' " And then the Cardinal spoke a little more about the greatness of the man whose anniversary they were met to celebrate and he ended: "Of such Christlike compassion and vision, of such childlike and courageous faith, the saints of God are made."

Those who were still children when Father Drumgoole died and those who came in later years to his Home have brought credit to the man who believed in them. His children have not failed his faith in them. The two little boys who had lived under the market and whom no other institution would take became two of the finest children in the Home and later made equally fine citizens.

The first two boys he educated to be priests were ordained shortly after his death. One, after some years of duty at Mount Loretto, was sent to Tuckahoe in Westchester, and there built a beautiful church and staffed its school with Sisters from the congregation whose members Father Drumgoole had begged long ago from Bishop Ryan. The other was for many years pastor of St. Peter's Church in Staten Island. Both wore the robes of domestic prelates.

Among the ranks of his alumni are boys who have become secular priests, Oblates, Passionists, Dominicans, Holy Cross Fathers, Jesuits; hardly a well-known order is without Mount Loretto boys in its ranks. From the famous Latin class under Mr. Kernan came boys who, after they left the classic retreat of their cottage, went to Dunwoodie and became priests.

The girls have not failed him either. Many have entered the Franciscan community which he brought to his Home and there are others who are Sisters of St. Joseph, Sisters of Mercy, Dominicans, Trappistines.

Brother Adrian of the Community of the Sacred Heart wrote of the Mission, "My heart goes out to the dear old

Home when I think of my blessings in its sheltering arms. It gave me a mother's love and a father's care." And Father William Fogarty, once a boy there, said, "If today I am able to stand at God's altar to offer Him the sacrifice of the Mass, all the credit must be given to the Mission of the Immaculate Virgin."

These are among the glowing examples of the results of training in the Home built by a man who had faith and hope and an incredible amount of charity. He made Mount Loretto, as a Commissioner of Charity was to say, "an outstanding example of what one fervent, energetic man can accomplish."

In 1940 the alumni planned their first formal reunion. Fifteen hundred attended with their wives and husbands and children. They were quite evidently a prosperous and happy group, among them lawyers, merchants, doctors, musicians, women in business life, mothers of children. They were a living answer to the question of what becomes of children raised in such an institution as the Mission. Do they become good citizens? These people were living proof that they do.

Often to his children Father Drumgoole had said, "You are American citizens. Be proud of it. Be faithful to God and you will be faithful to your country." And the many who on that day crowded the lovely church of his planning, where stood the flag of their country and the flag of their Church, were proof that his teachings are living still. They were proof, too, that the true glory of the Mission of the Immaculate Virgin is not in its size or its buildings or its fine program, but in the hearts of the countless children who knew it as a home where they had found love, a home to which they could return in sorrow or in joy, in defeat or in victory.

At the fiftieth anniversary of his death Monsignor Lavelle had said that Father Drumgoole was among the giants like St. Paul and St. Vincent and Father Damien, "whom every once in a while God sends into the world." That was very true and, like them, he had his feet firmly fixed on the earth while his mind and his heart had broken through the clouds to reach heaven.

And one more thing is surely true of him today—that where he walks in heaven innumerable children are clinging to his long black cloak.

Bibliography

Adams, William: *Ireland and Irish Immigration.* Yale University Press, New Haven, 1932.

Bayley, James Roosevelt: *Brief Sketch of the Early History of the Catholic Church.* Catholic Publications Society, New York, 1870.

Brace, Charles Loring: *Short Sermons to Newsboys.* Scribner's, New York, 1854.

Carty, Mother M. Peter, O.S.U.: *Old St. Patrick's Cathedral,* United States Catholic Historical Society, New York, 1947.

Crimmins, John D.: *Saint Patrick's Day.* Privately printed, 1902.

Davis, W. T.: *Staten Island and Its People.* Lewis Historical Publishing Company, New York, 1930.

Dougherty, James E.: *Day Book,* years from 1879 to 1889 (manuscript).

Emmet, T. H.: "Irish Immigration." *Journal of American Historical Society,* volume 2, 1899.

Flynn, Rev. Richard A.: "Reverend Father Drumgoole." Three articles, *Our Lady of Perpetual Help,* New York City, October to December 1939.

Folks, Homer: *Care of Destitute and Neglected Children.* Macmillan Company, New York, 1902.

Jacoby, Rev. George Paul: *Catholic Child Care in 19th Century New York.* Catholic University of America Press, Washington, D. C., 1941.

Lewis, Samuel: *Topographical Dictionary of Ireland.*

Maguire, John F., M.P.: *The Irish in America.* S. Lewis and Co., London, 1840.

McColgan, Rev. Daniel: *A Century of Charity.* Bruce Publishing Company, Milwaukee, 1951.

McNichol, Rev. F. P.: *Life of Father Drumgoole*. Mount Loretto Press, Staten Island, 1894.

McKey, J. P.: *History of Niagara University*. Privately printed. 1931.

Marquess of Cress: *Lord Rosebery*. John Murray, London, 1931.

McGee, Thomas: *History of the Irish Settlers*. Patrick Donahoe, Boston, 1852.

Shea, John Gilmary: *Catholic Churches of New York City*. L. G. Goulding and Co., New York, 1878.

"What Can Be Done for Our Orphans?" *American Catholic Quarterly Review*, January 1866.

Sister Marie Eucharia, O.S.F.: *Rev. John C. Drumgoole*. Mount Loretto Press, Staten Island, n.d.

Taraffe, Thomas Gaffney. "Archbishop Hughes." *Catholic Review*, 1881.

Catholic Encyclopedia
Columbia Encyclopedia
Freeman's Journal
Mount Loretto Messenger
Note Books and Letters—City House
Pamphlet: *Memorial of St. Xarier's Church*, New York, 1882
Souvenir Album: Centennial Anniversary of N. Y. Archdiocese 1808–1908
The Homeless Child
The Truth Teller

Index

Date Due

Demco 293-5